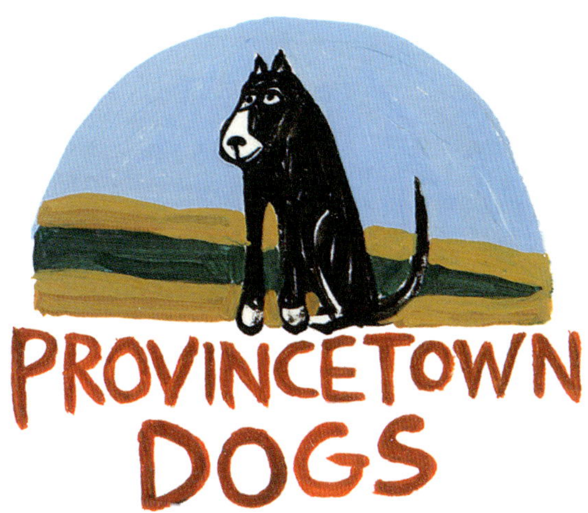
PROVINCETOWN
DOGS

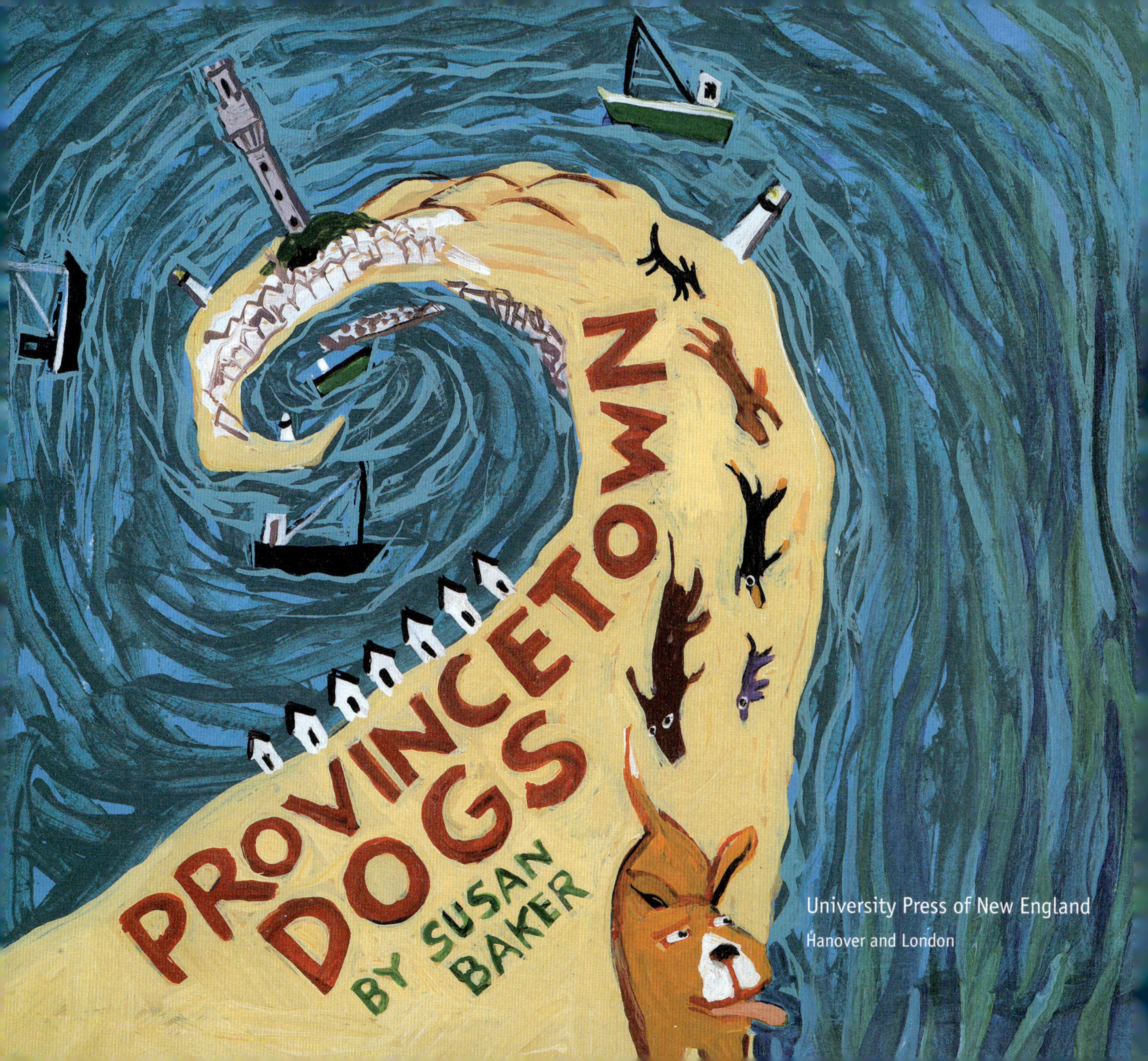

University Press of New England
Hanover and London

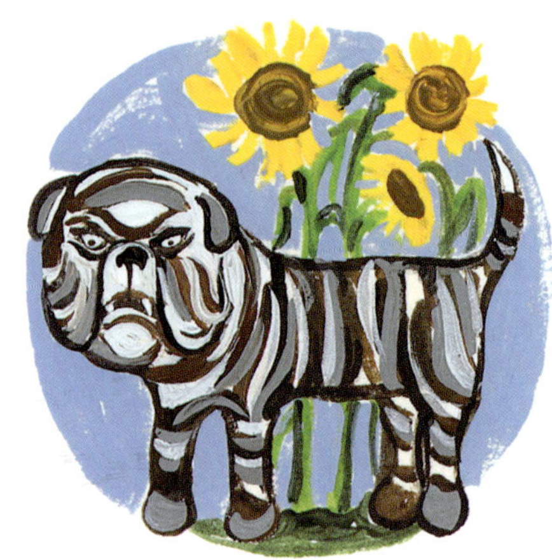

University Press of New England

Hanover, NH 03755

Printed in Singapore

5 4 3 2 1

Library of Congress Cataloging-in-Publication Data

Baker, Susan

Provincetown dogs / by Susan Baker

p. cm.

ISBN 1-58465-037-0

1. Dogs—Fiction. 2. Provincetown (Mass.)—Fiction

PS3552.A4347 P76 2000

813'.54 21 99–44080

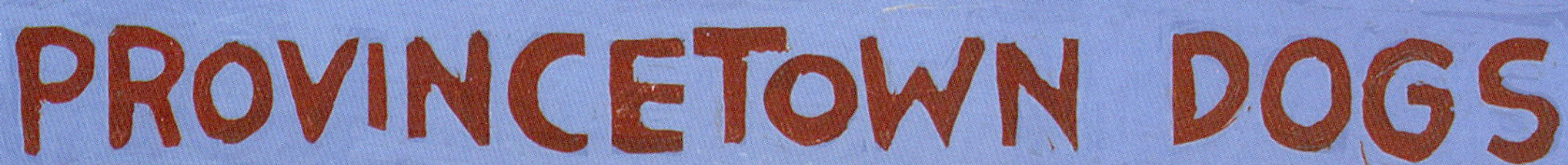

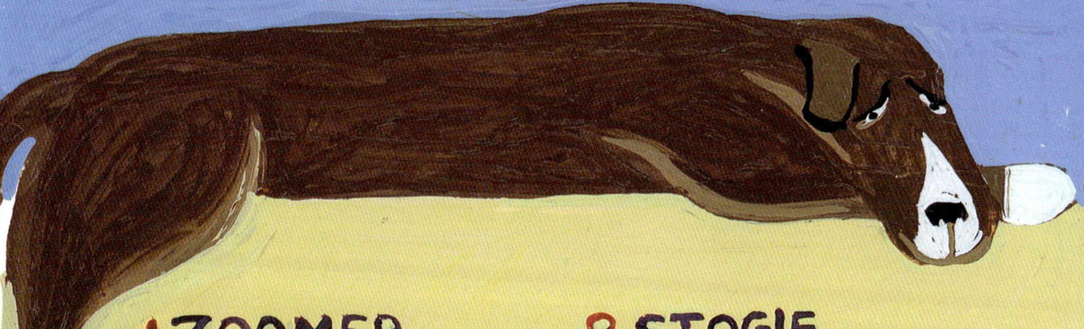

1 ZOOMER
2 BUSTER
3 DOGGIE
4 DOGETTE
5 ROMEO
6 HARRY
7 TEDDY
8 STOGIE
9 JOHNNY LOW-DOWN
10 OLD MR BOSTON
11 PIE
12 ABIGAIL
13 TAR
14. FATSO + SKINNY

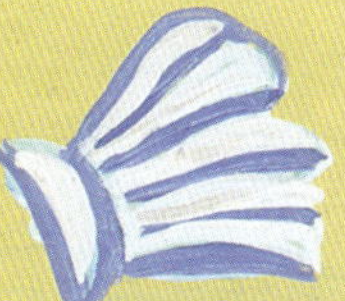

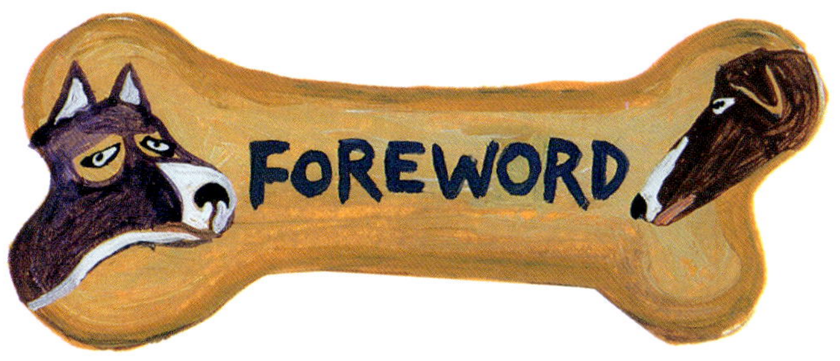

In one of the old cemeteries in Provincetown there is a statue of a dog sitting vigil over its master's grave. It's near the site of the old railroad station, now torn down, and in the shade of the newer Pilgrim Monument, in a town that was once a bustling whaling port, then a fishing village, an artists colony, and a summer resort. This beautiful marker points to one constant in Provincetown life through many eras of change—the love of dogs.

Susan Baker's tableaux cut across all sizes, shapes, colors, and breeds of dogs, and focuses on their personalities. That is what we bond with, and how we recall them. There's a built-in sadness to having dogs, in that we usually outlive them. All dog lovers in their lifetimes will compile their own list of dogs they have known and loved. Each is distinguished by his or her personality, and the foibles and antics that displayed it.

Susan Baker's paintings and text go together so perfectly there is no step up or down from one to the other. They are equally immediate and fresh, heartfelt and unstudied, yet smart and full of wit. These lively portraits leave you tingling like a big sloppy lick from a dog.

Although we call ourselves their owners, and masters, it is to them we look for lessons in freedom, and to their uncanny ability to relax, their exemplary forgiveness, and their capacity for joy.

Though no dog on its own will ever read this book, no doubt many will have it read to them while they are trying to sleep, and have the pictures shoved under their noses for inspection. Being of superior intelligence and kind hearts, they will probably bear these interruptions with good will, or at most a stage growl, sensing our desire to share their uncomplicated happiness.

It's this joy we envy and that Susan Baker captures in this remarkable book.

Keith Althaus

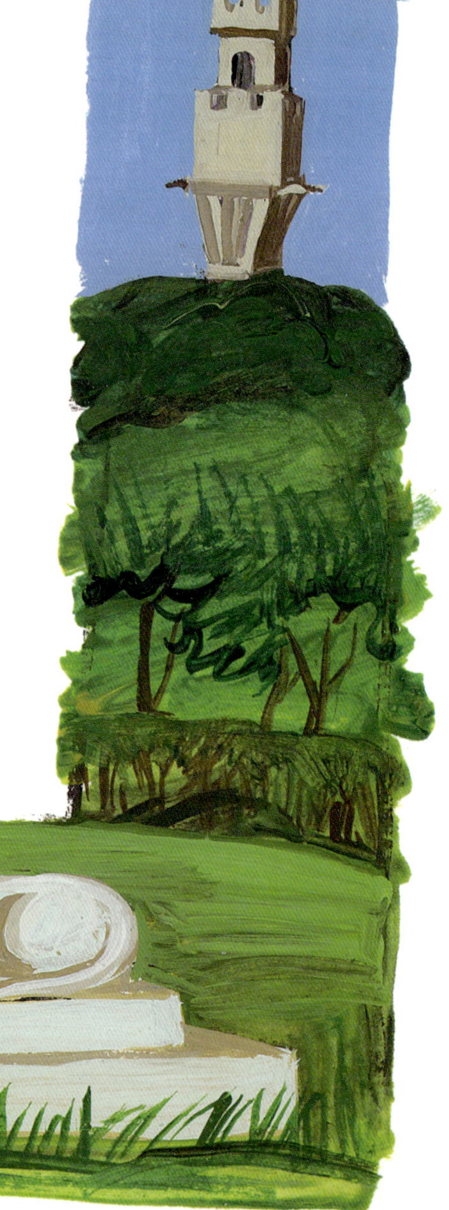

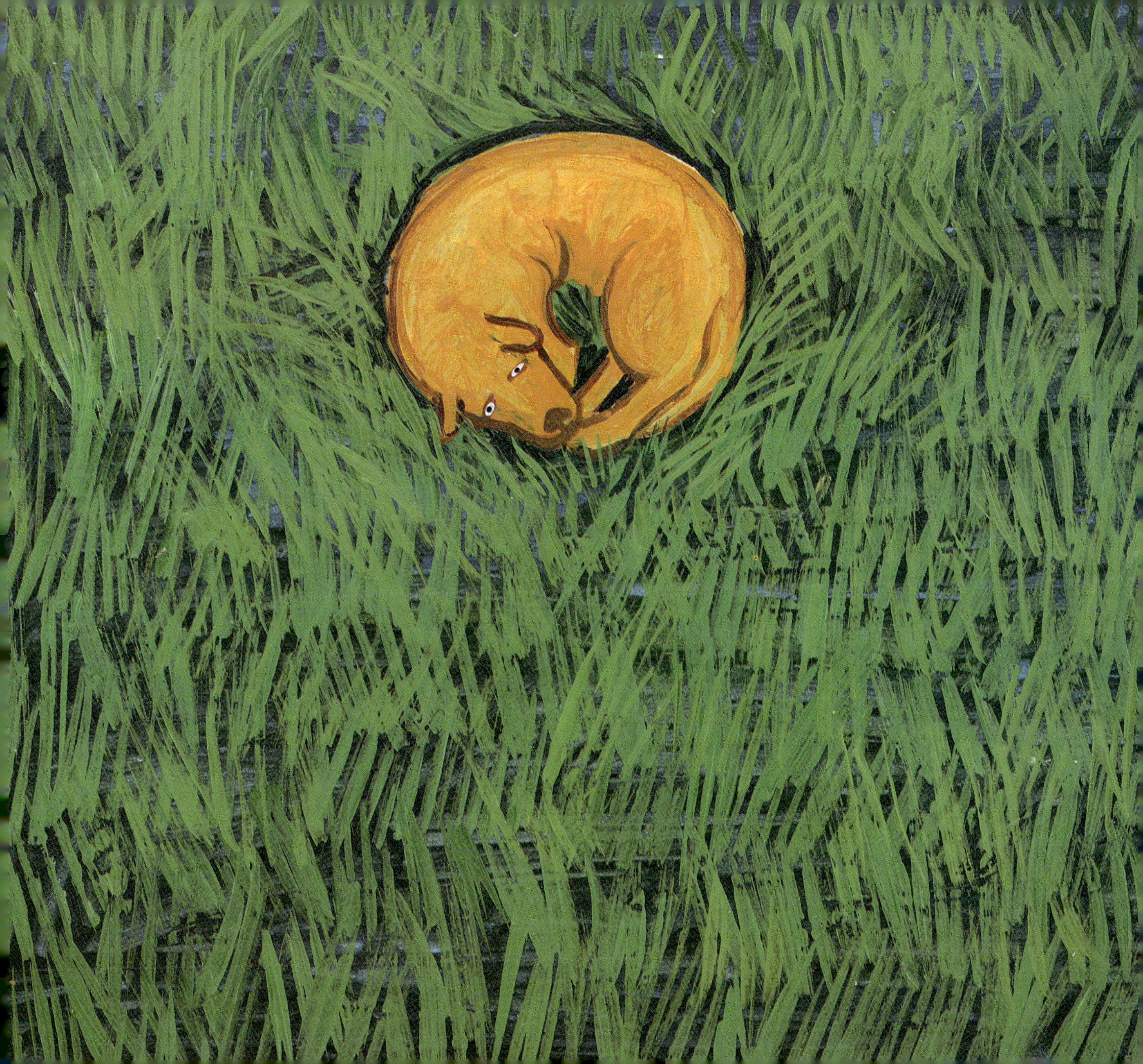

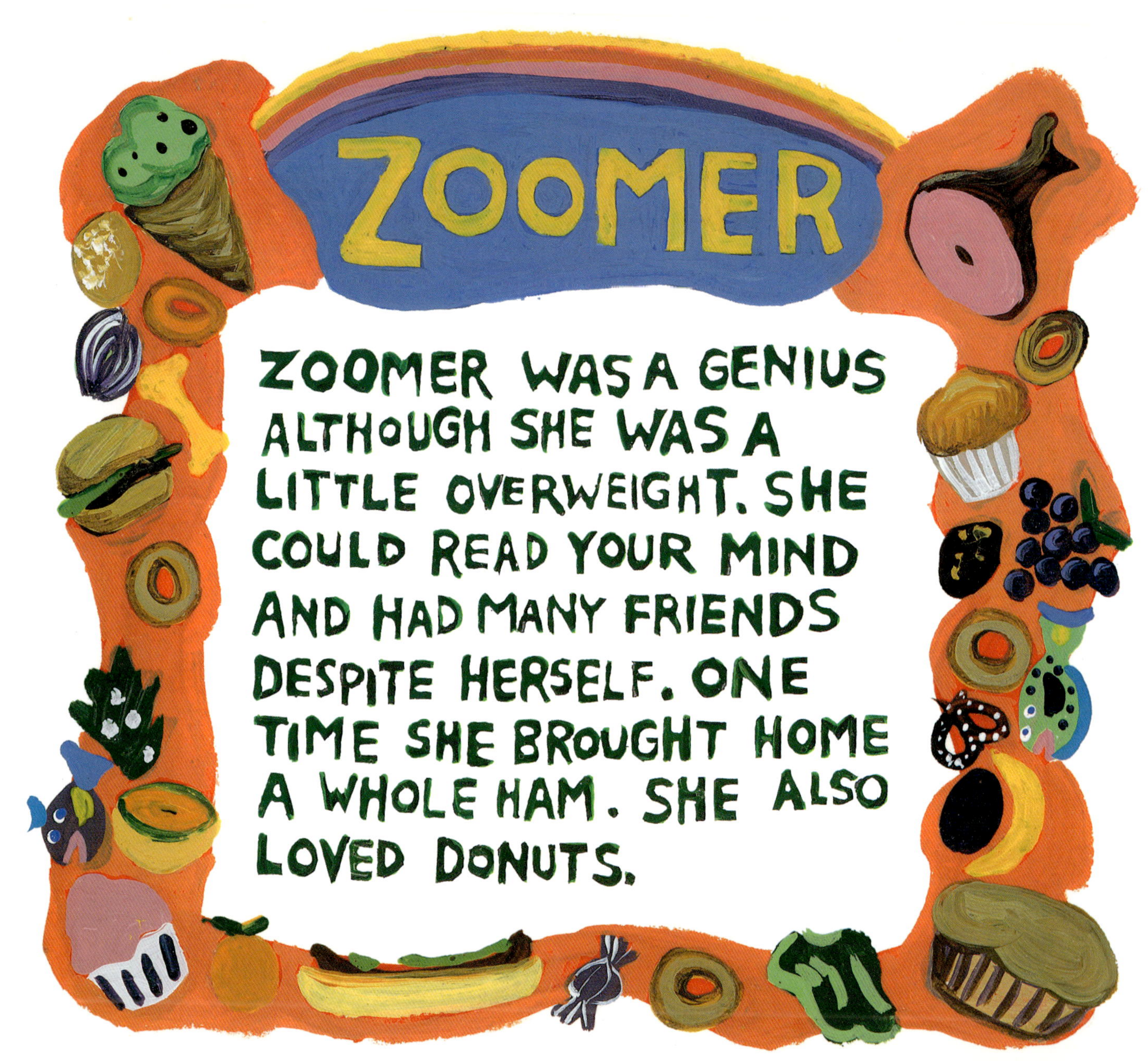
ZOOMER
ZOOMER WAS A GENIUS ALTHOUGH SHE WAS A LITTLE OVERWEIGHT. SHE COULD READ YOUR MIND AND HAD MANY FRIENDS DESPITE HERSELF. ONE TIME SHE BROUGHT HOME A WHOLE HAM. SHE ALSO LOVED DONUTS.

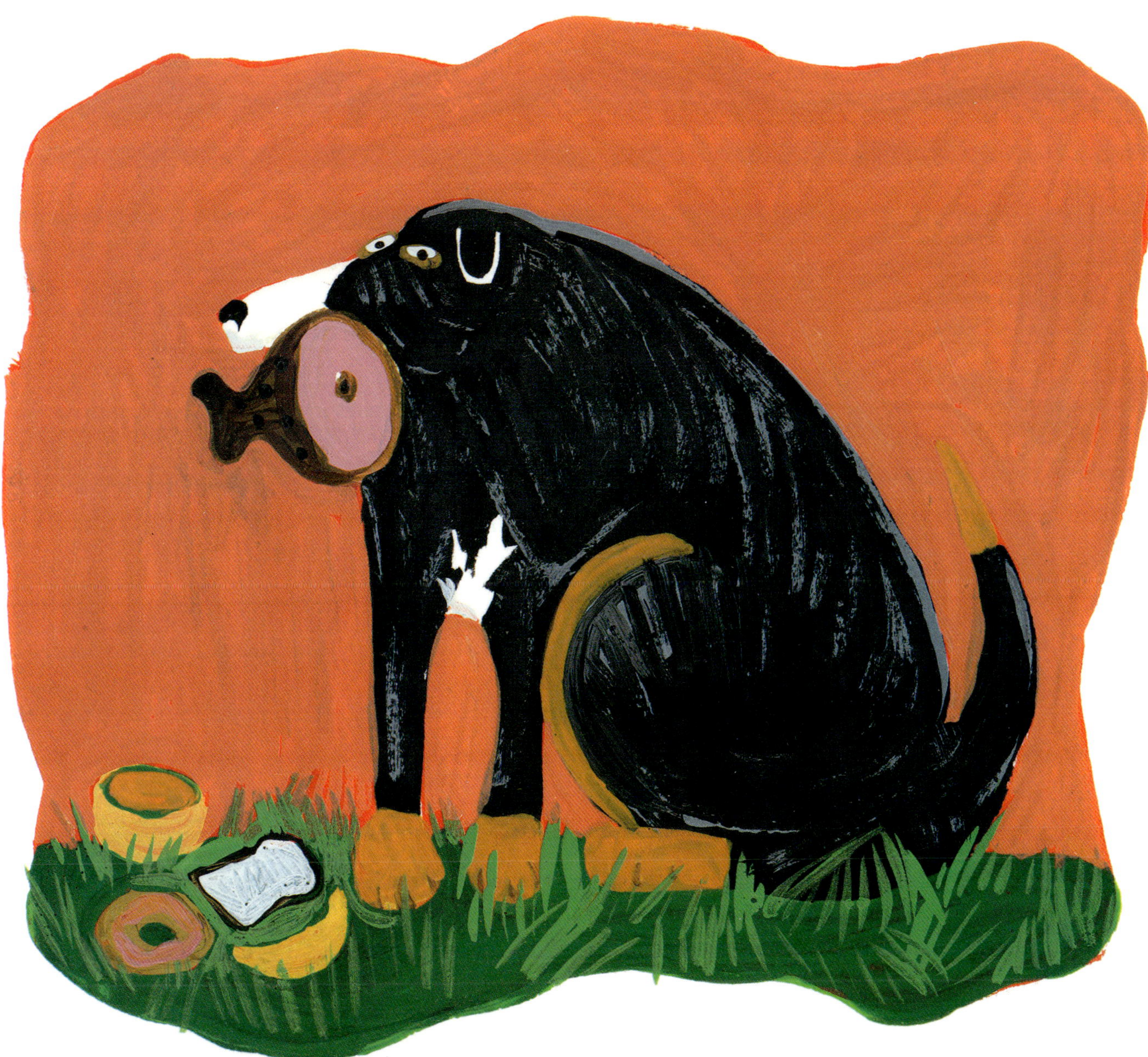

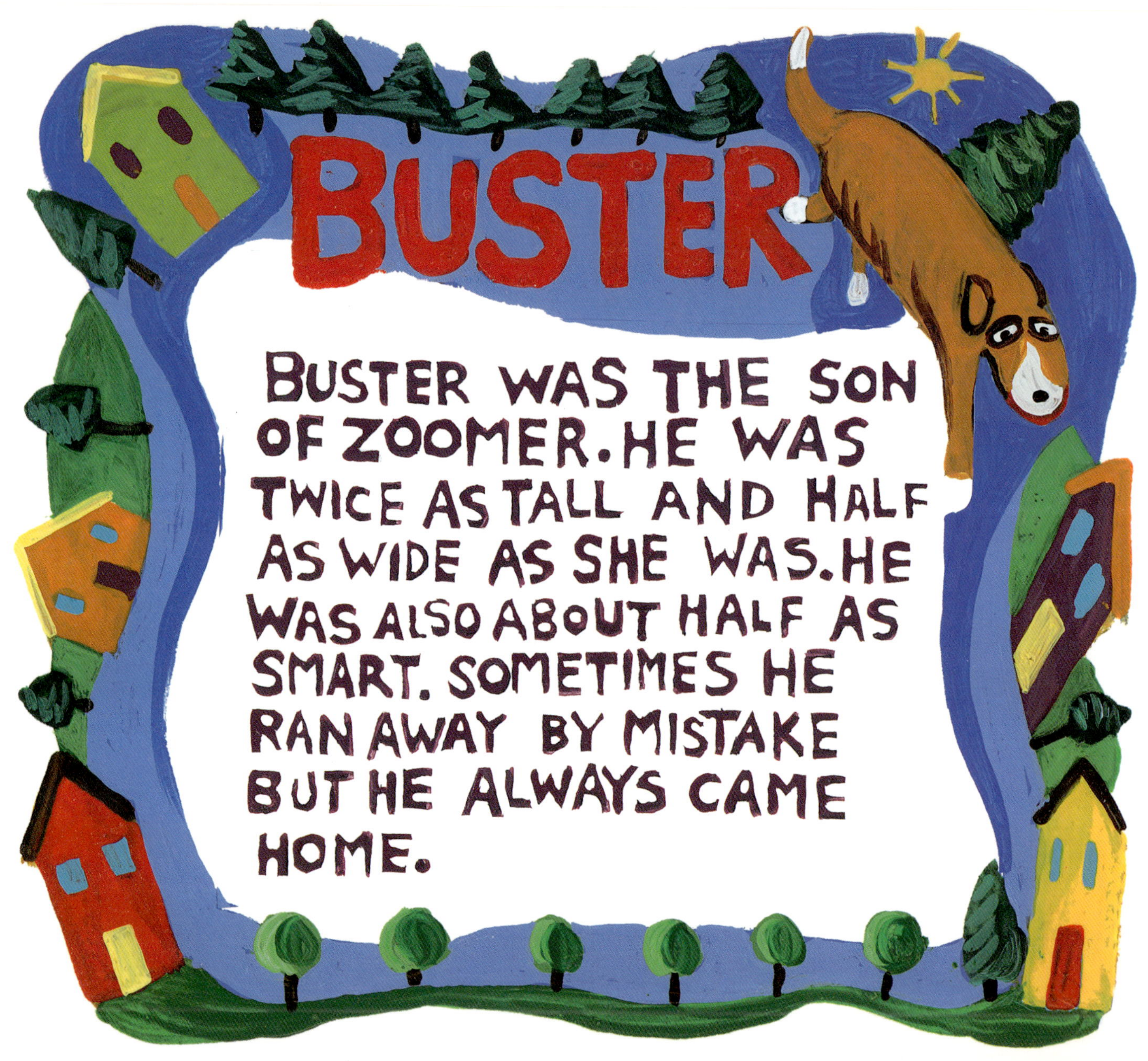
BUSTER
BUSTER WAS THE SON OF ZOOMER. HE WAS TWICE AS TALL AND HALF AS WIDE AS SHE WAS. HE WAS ALSO ABOUT HALF AS SMART. SOMETIMES HE RAN AWAY BY MISTAKE BUT HE ALWAYS CAME HOME.

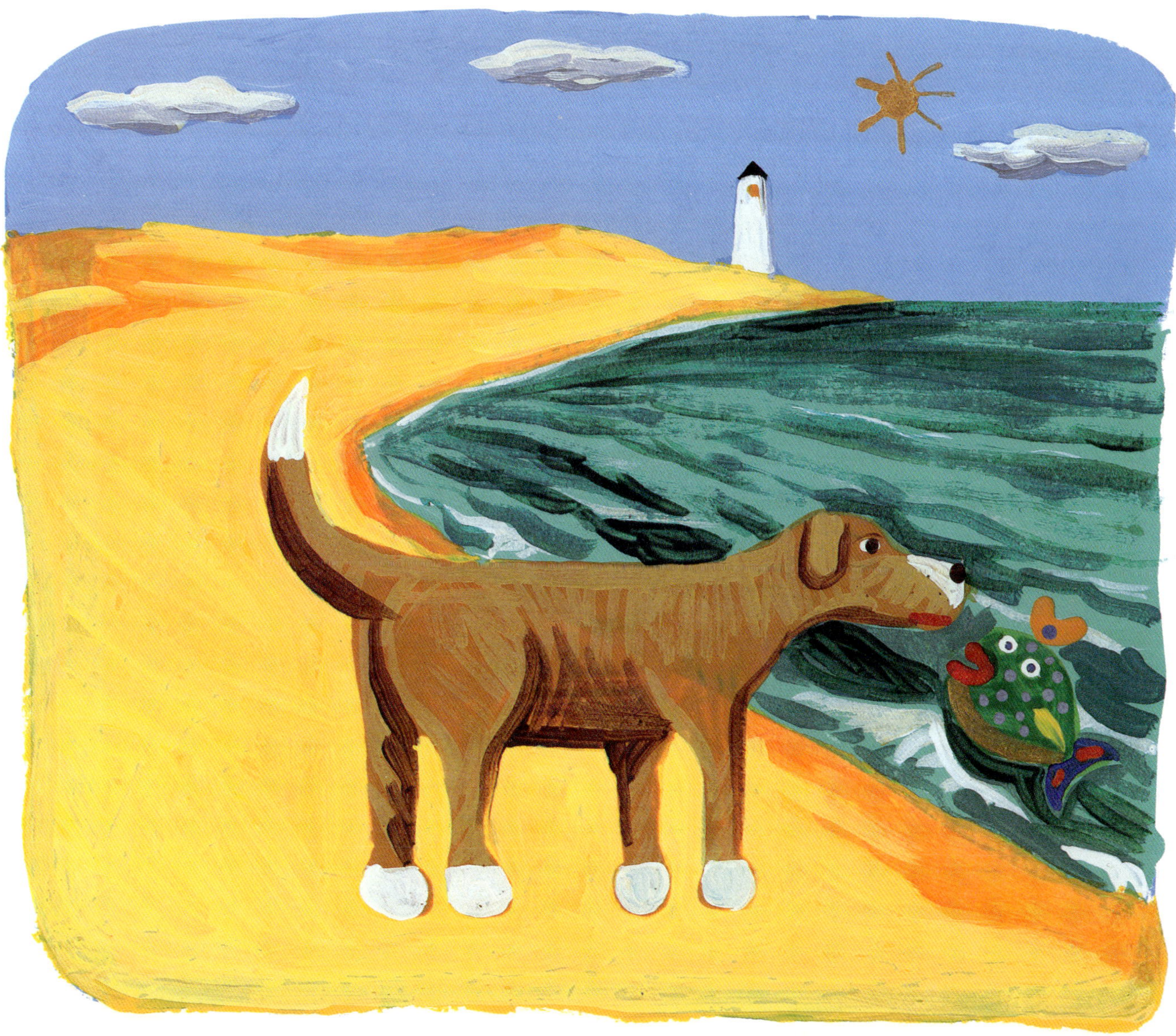

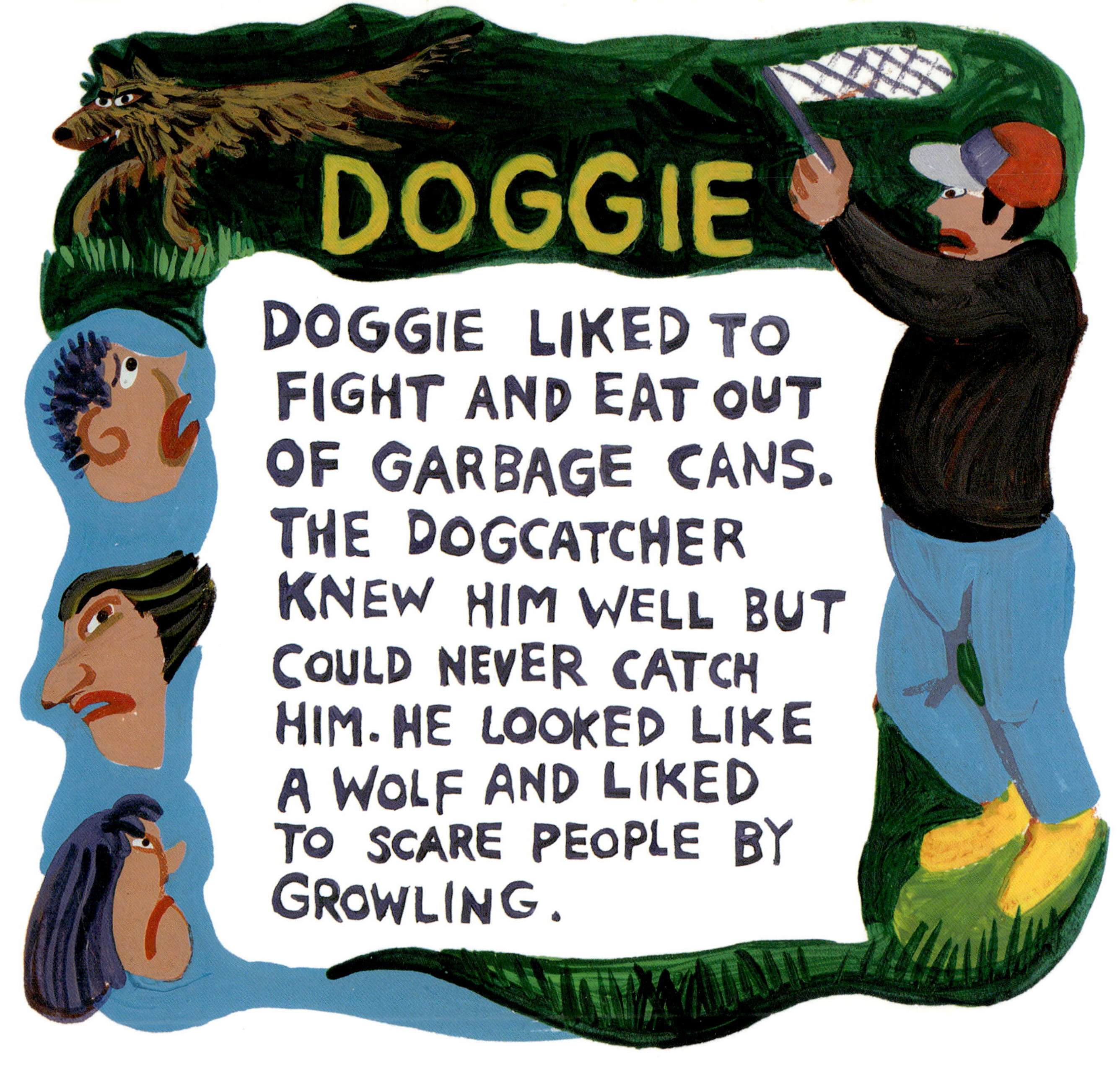
DOGGIE
DOGGIE LIKED TO FIGHT AND EAT OUT OF GARBAGE CANS. THE DOGCATCHER KNEW HIM WELL BUT COULD NEVER CATCH HIM. HE LOOKED LIKE A WOLF AND LIKED TO SCARE PEOPLE BY GROWLING.

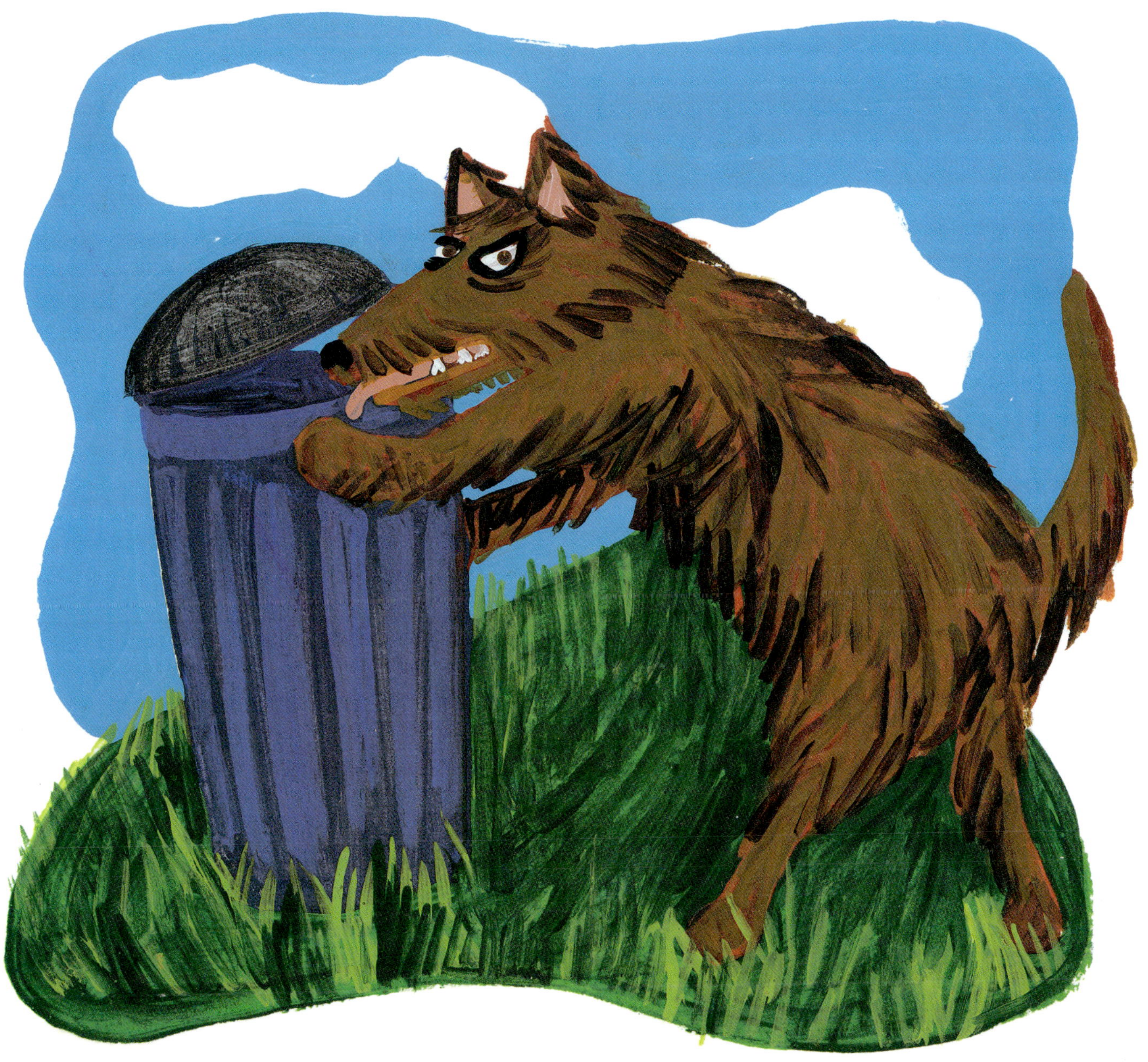

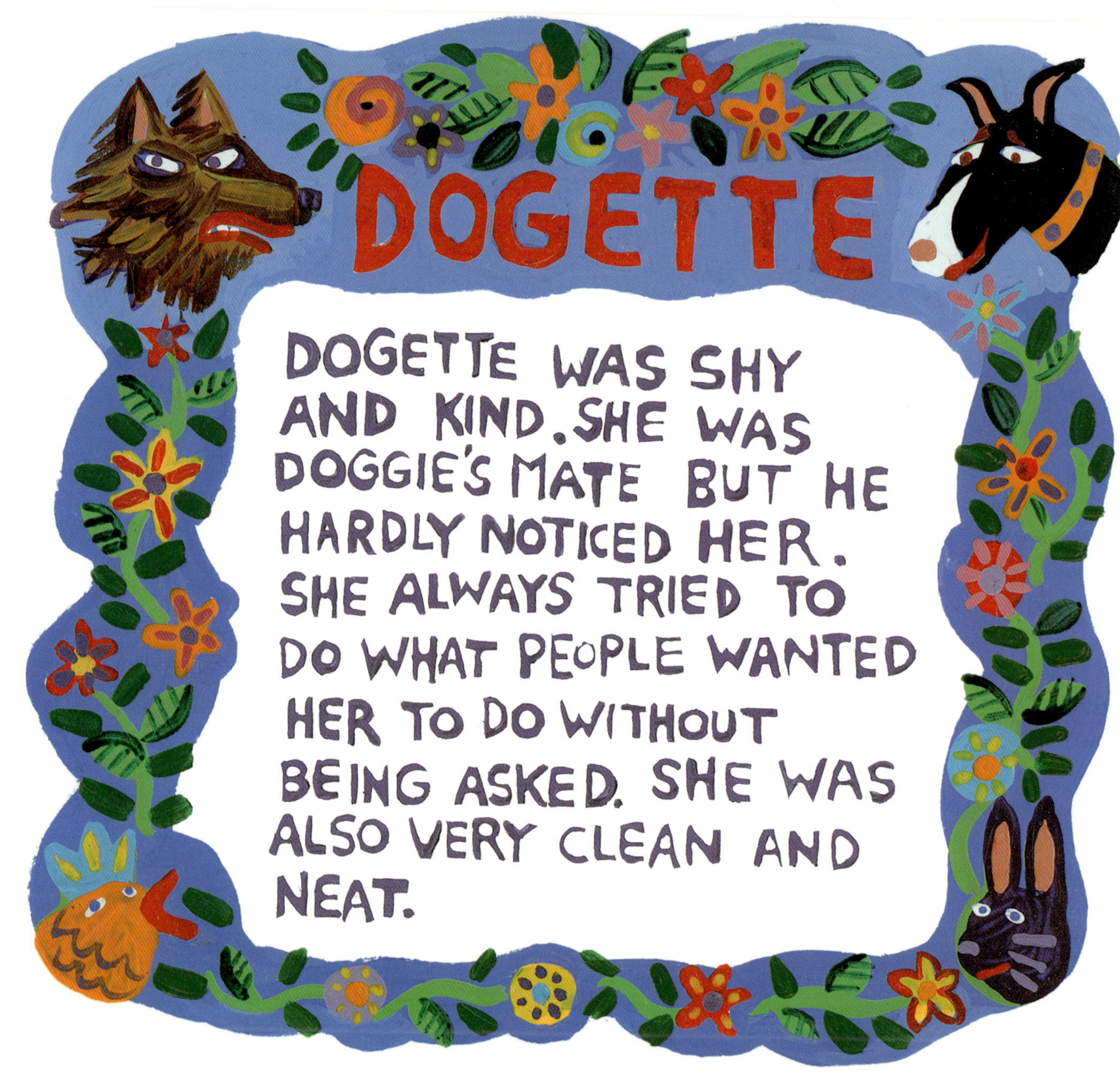
DOGETTE
DOGETTE WAS SHY AND KIND. SHE WAS DOGGIE'S MATE BUT HE HARDLY NOTICED HER. SHE ALWAYS TRIED TO DO WHAT PEOPLE WANTED HER TO DO WITHOUT BEING ASKED. SHE WAS ALSO VERY CLEAN AND NEAT.

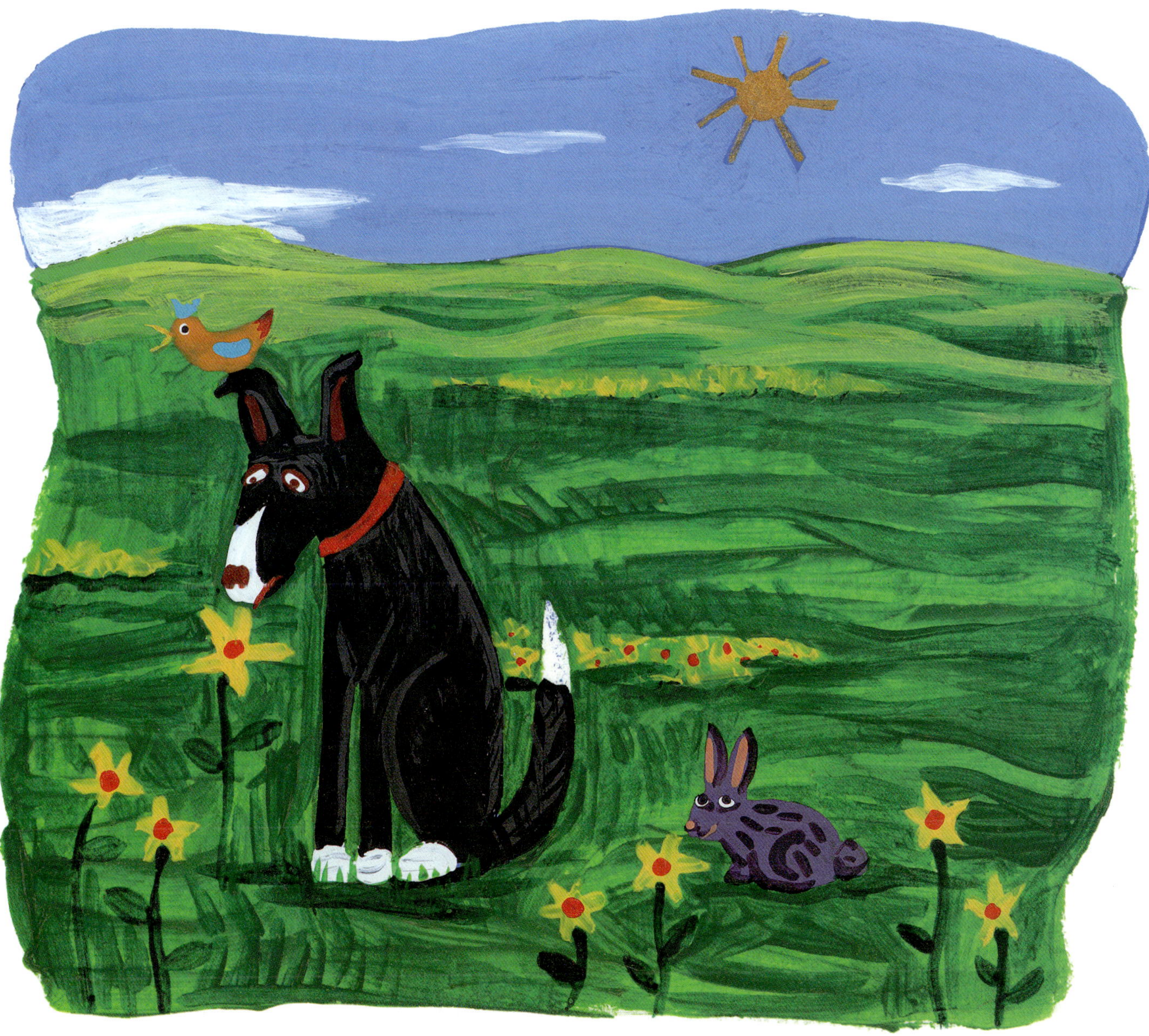

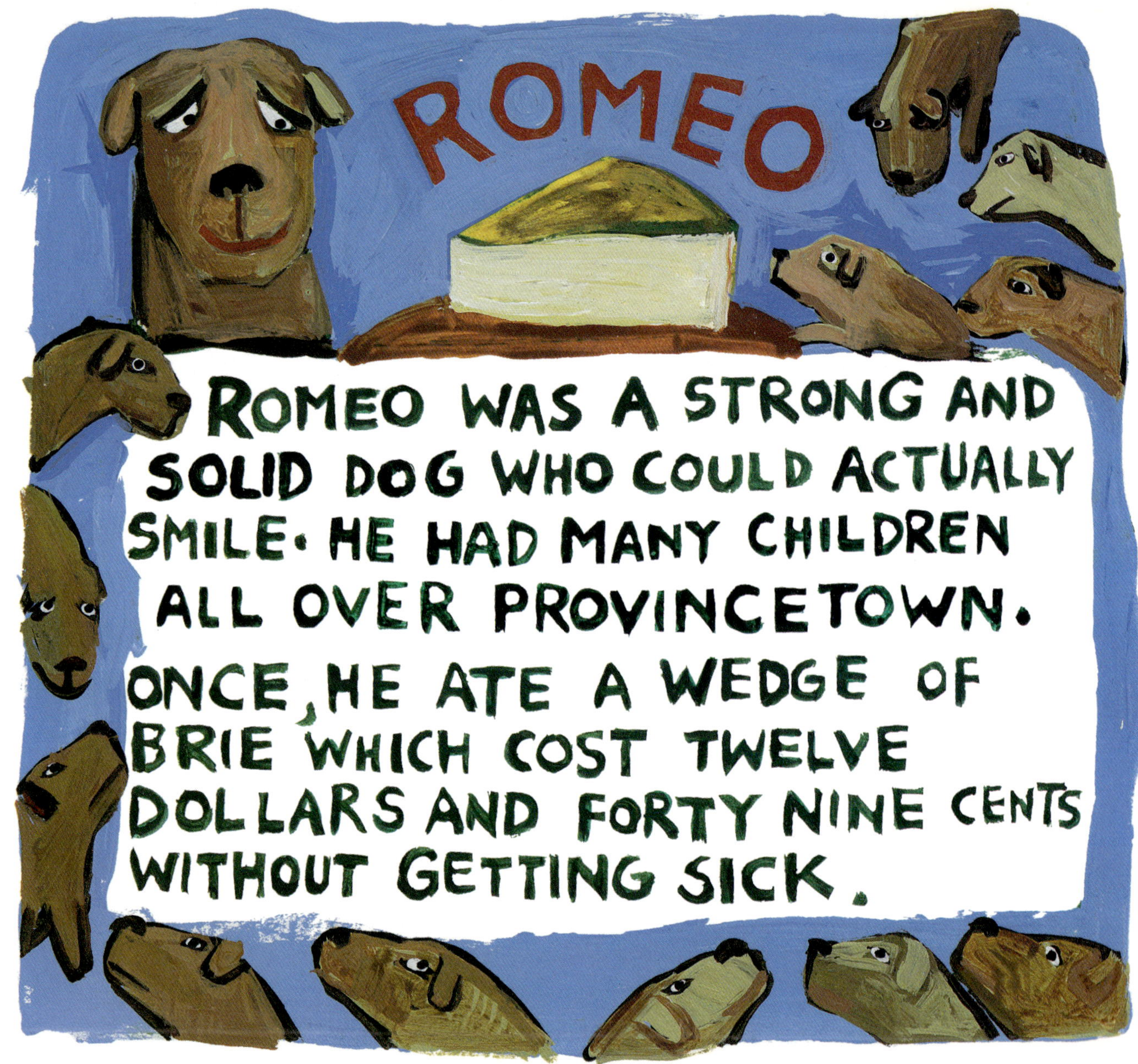
ROMEO
ROMEO WAS A STRONG AND SOLID DOG WHO COULD ACTUALLY SMILE. HE HAD MANY CHILDREN ALL OVER PROVINCETOWN.
ONCE, HE ATE A WEDGE OF BRIE WHICH COST TWELVE DOLLARS AND FORTY NINE CENTS WITHOUT GETTING SICK.

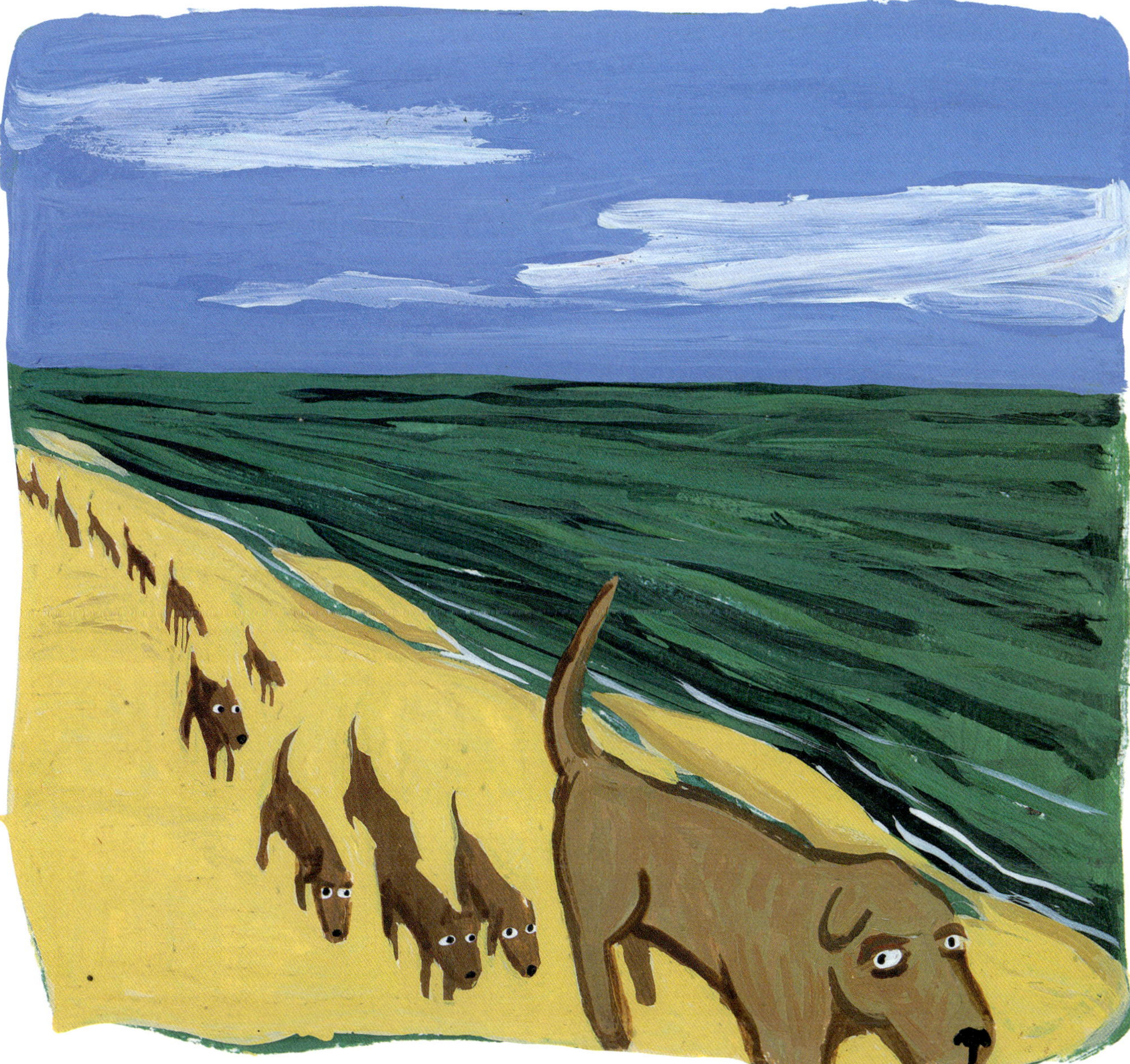

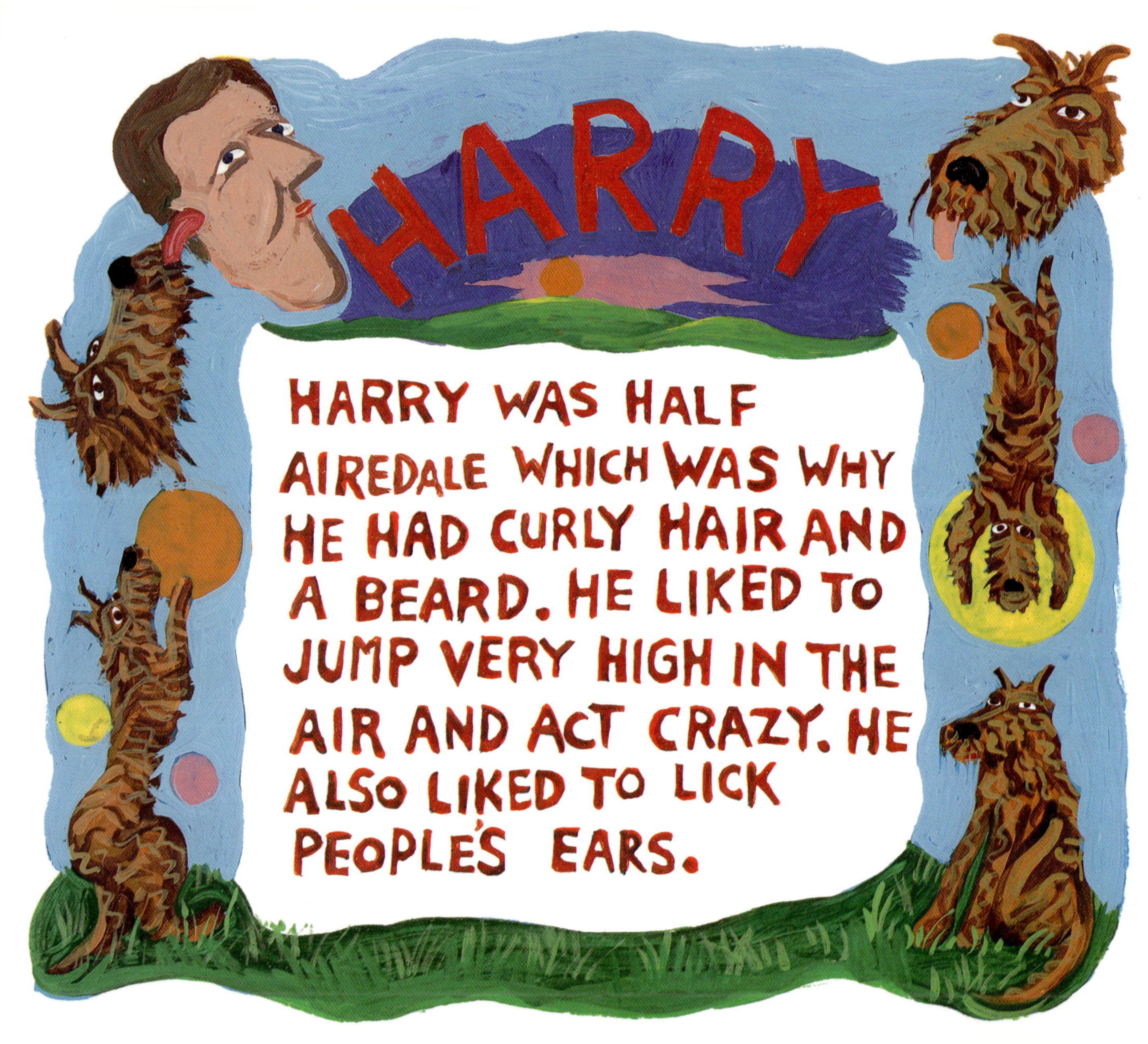
HARRY
HARRY WAS HALF AIREDALE WHICH WAS WHY HE HAD CURLY HAIR AND A BEARD. HE LIKED TO JUMP VERY HIGH IN THE AIR AND ACT CRAZY. HE ALSO LIKED TO LICK PEOPLE'S EARS.

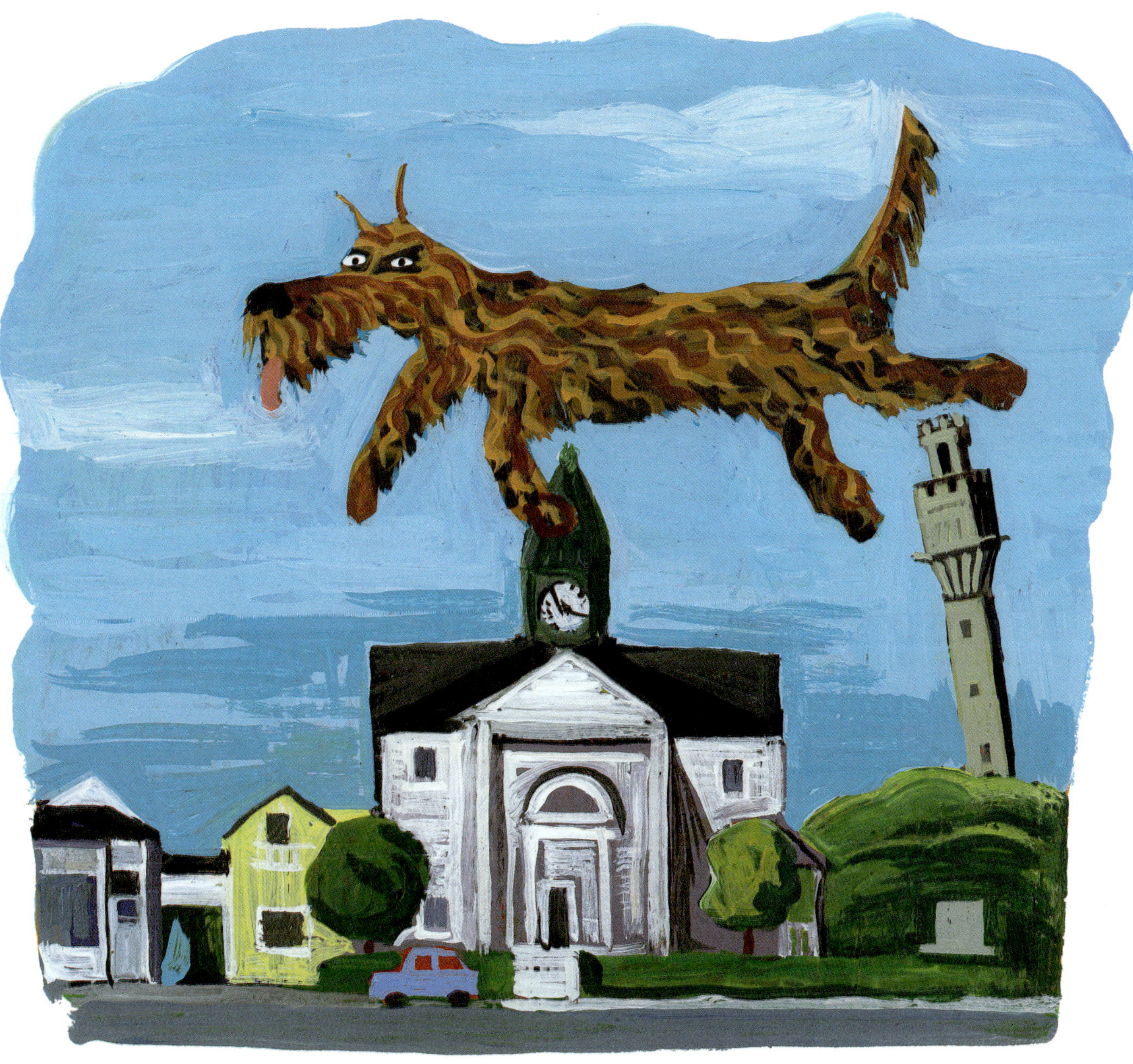

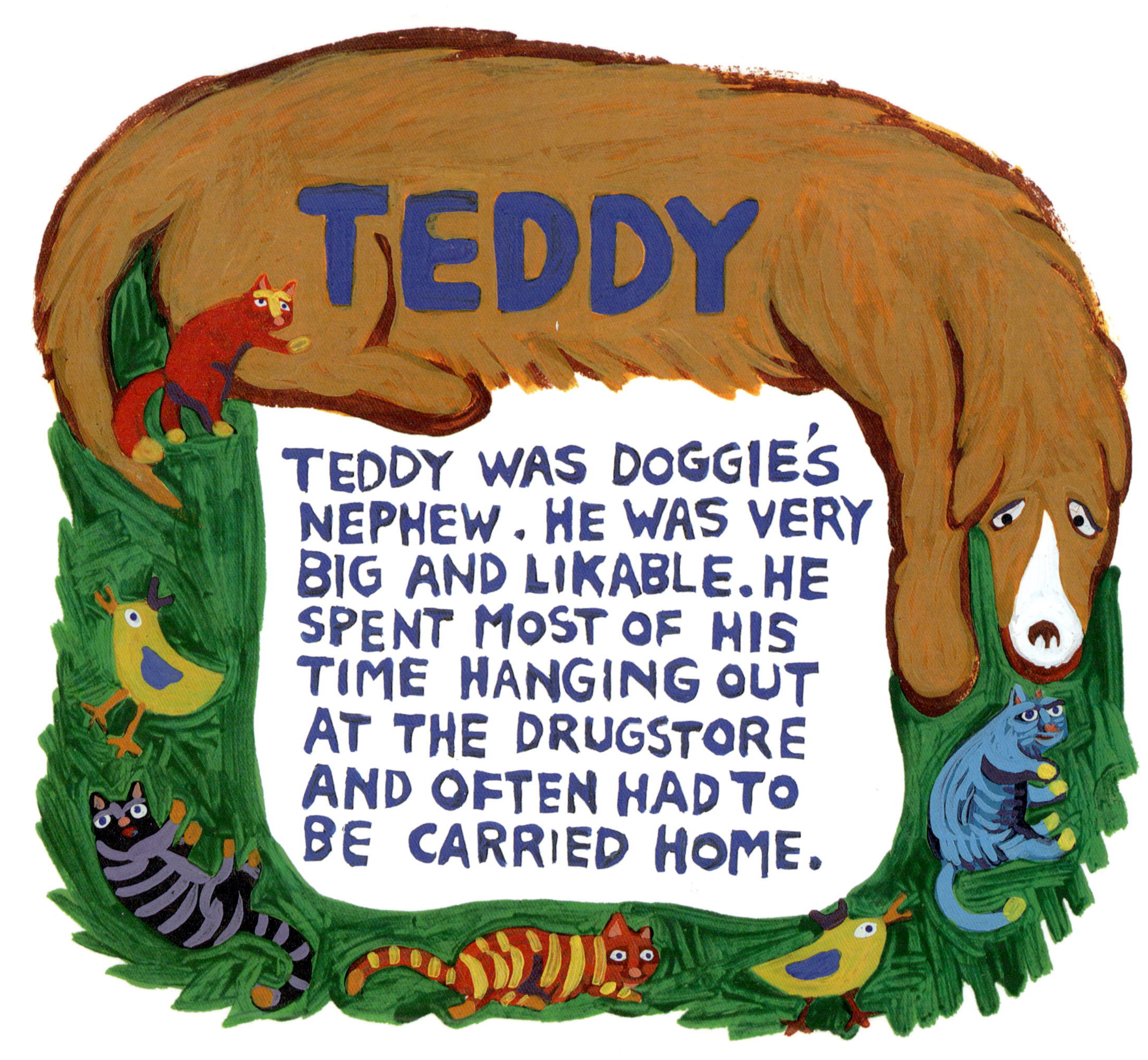
TEDDY
TEDDY WAS DOGGIE'S NEPHEW. HE WAS VERY BIG AND LIKABLE. HE SPENT MOST OF HIS TIME HANGING OUT AT THE DRUGSTORE AND OFTEN HAD TO BE CARRIED HOME.

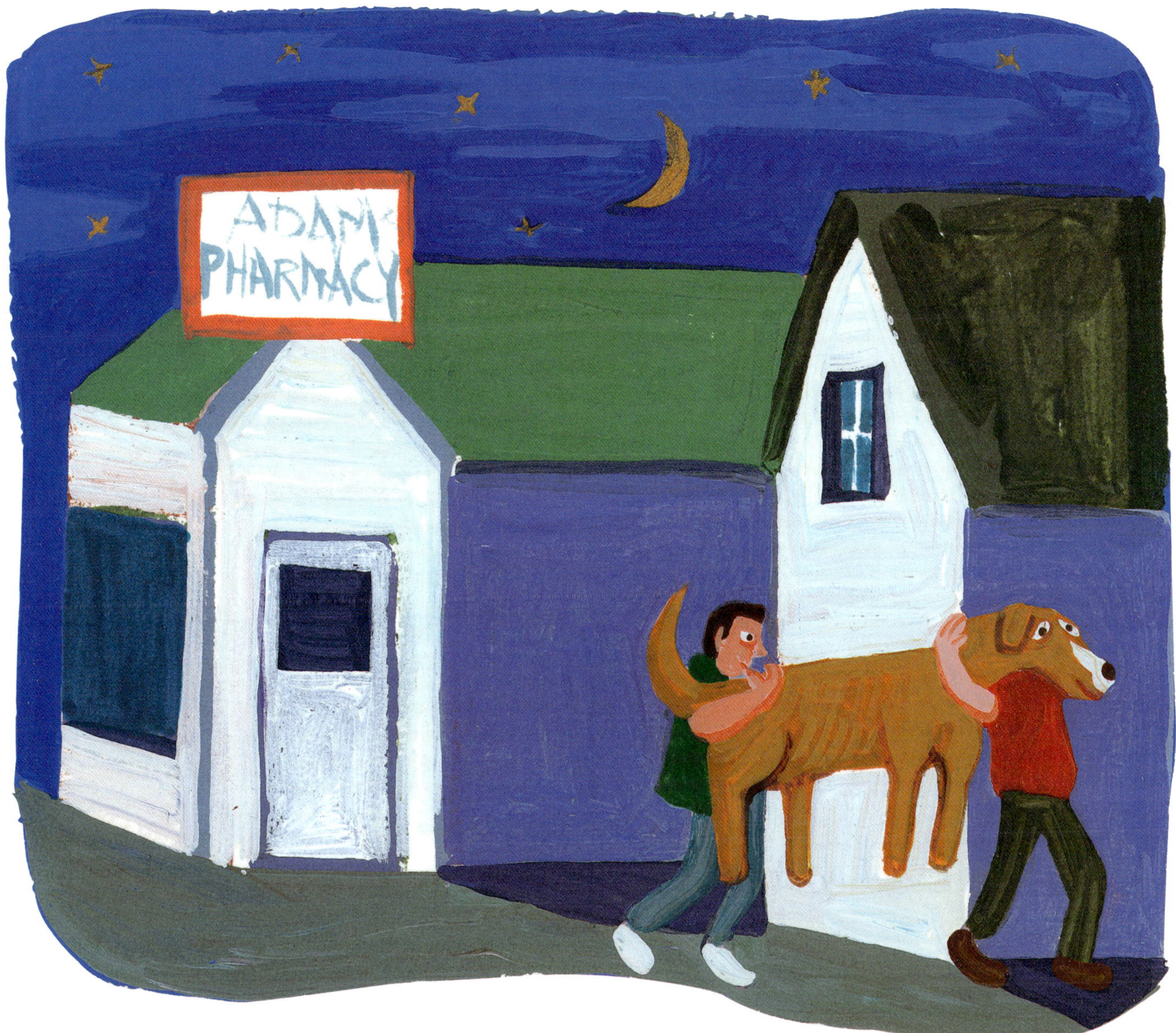
ADAM
PHARMACY

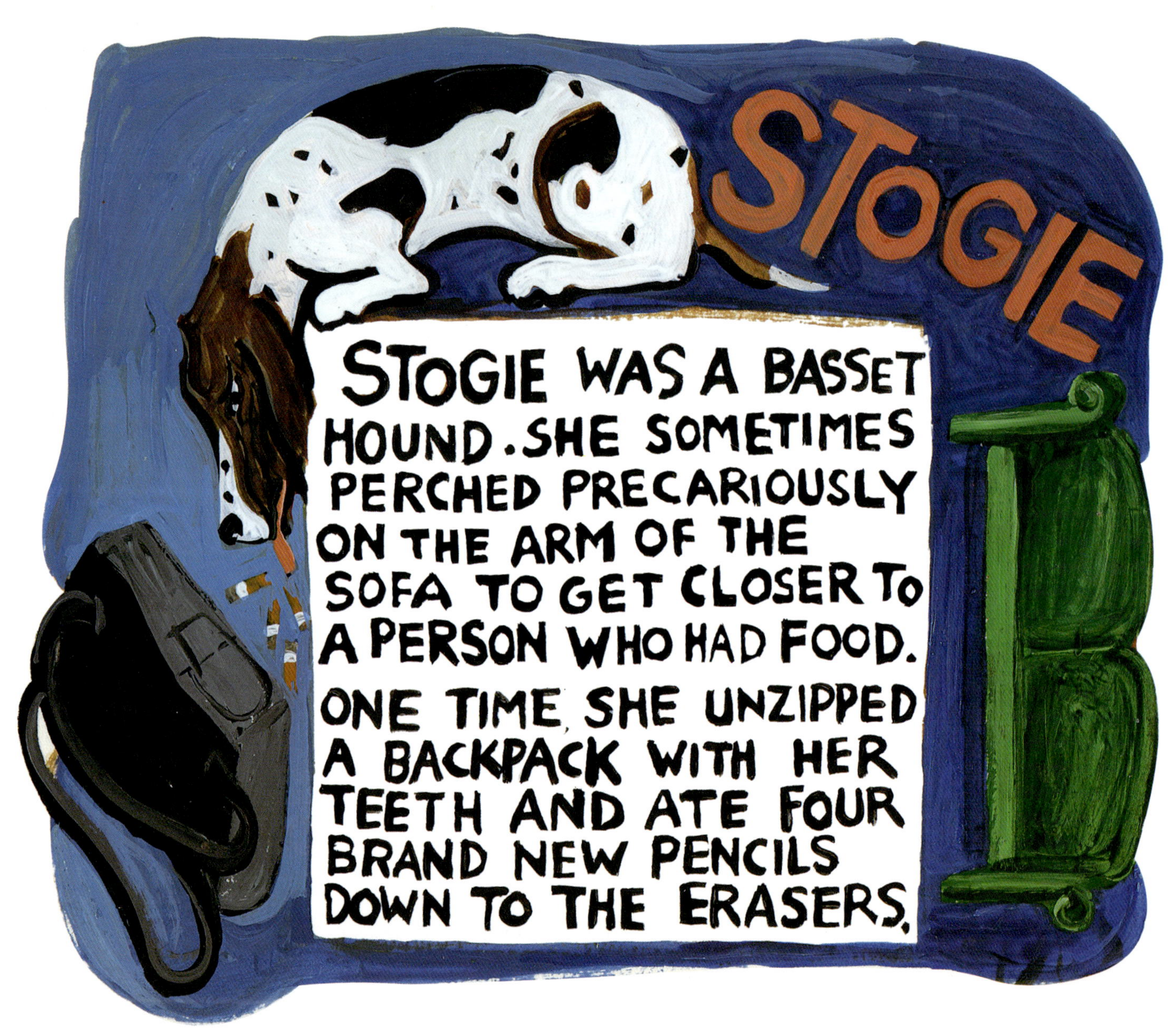
STOGIE
STOGIE WAS A BASSET HOUND. SHE SOMETIMES PERCHED PRECARIOUSLY ON THE ARM OF THE SOFA TO GET CLOSER TO A PERSON WHO HAD FOOD.
ONE TIME, SHE UNZIPPED A BACKPACK WITH HER TEETH AND ATE FOUR BRAND NEW PENCILS DOWN TO THE ERASERS.

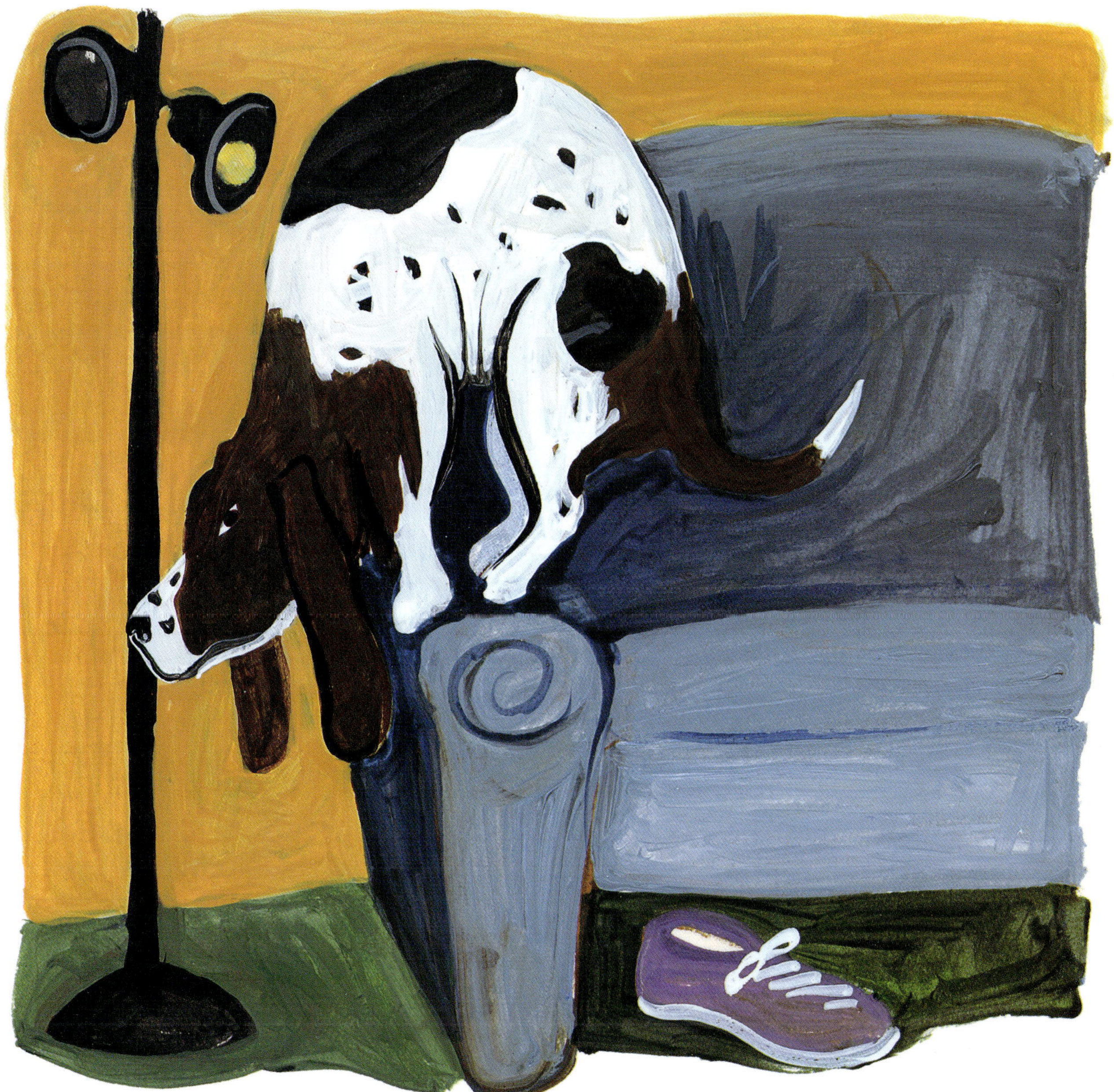

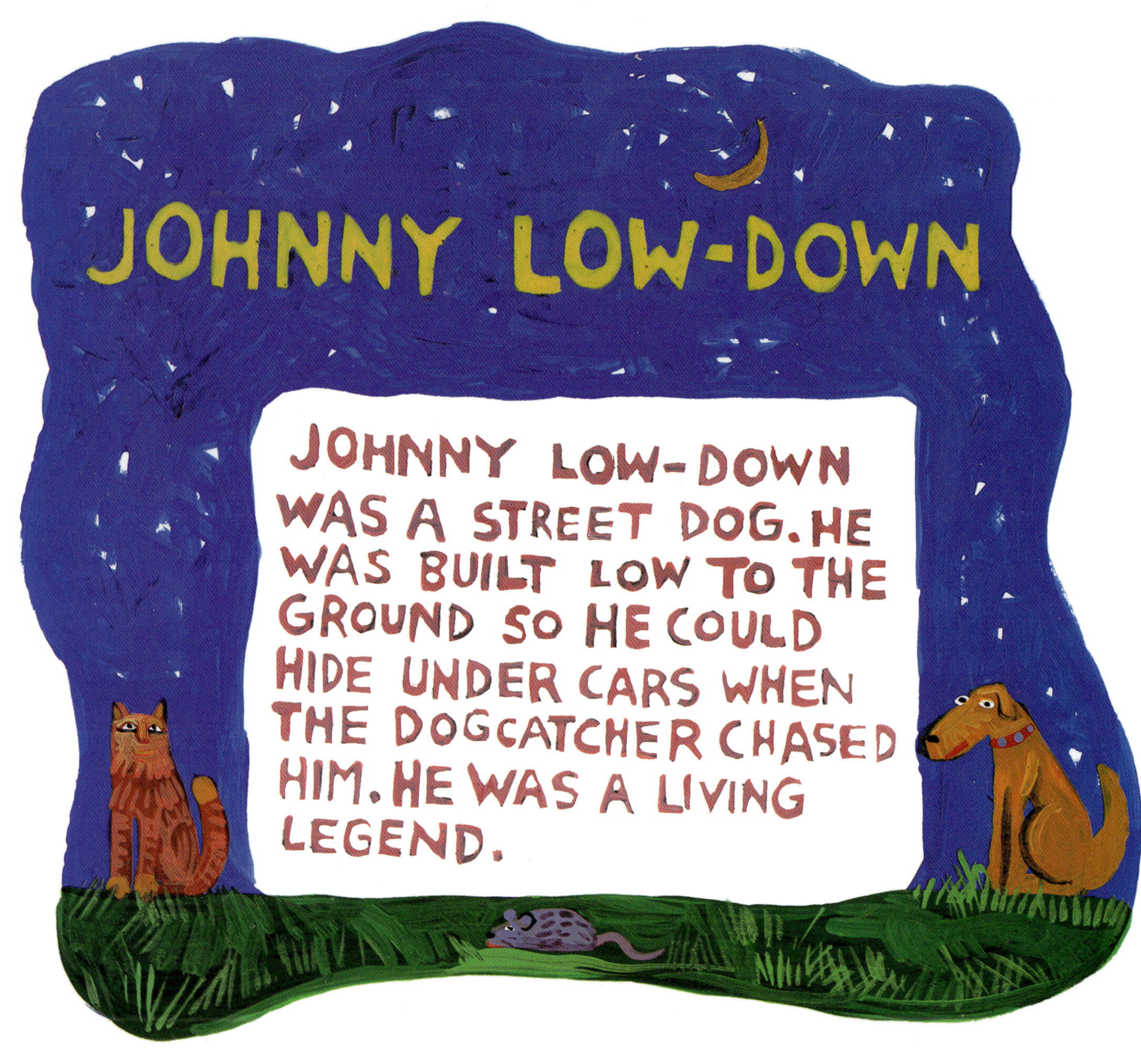
JOHNNY LOW-DOWN
JOHNNY LOW-DOWN WAS A STREET DOG. HE WAS BUILT LOW TO THE GROUND SO HE COULD HIDE UNDER CARS WHEN THE DOGCATCHER CHASED HIM. HE WAS A LIVING LEGEND.

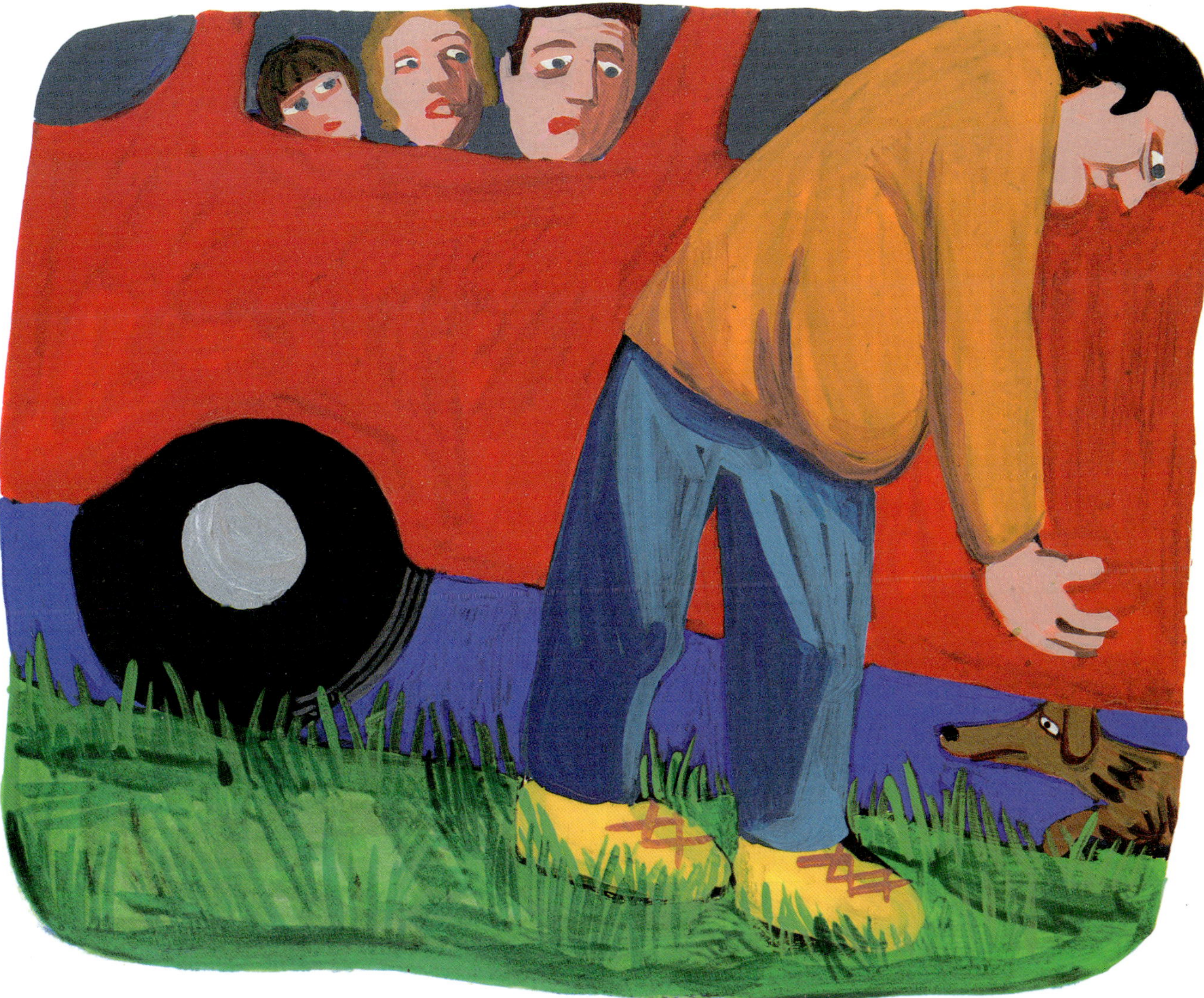

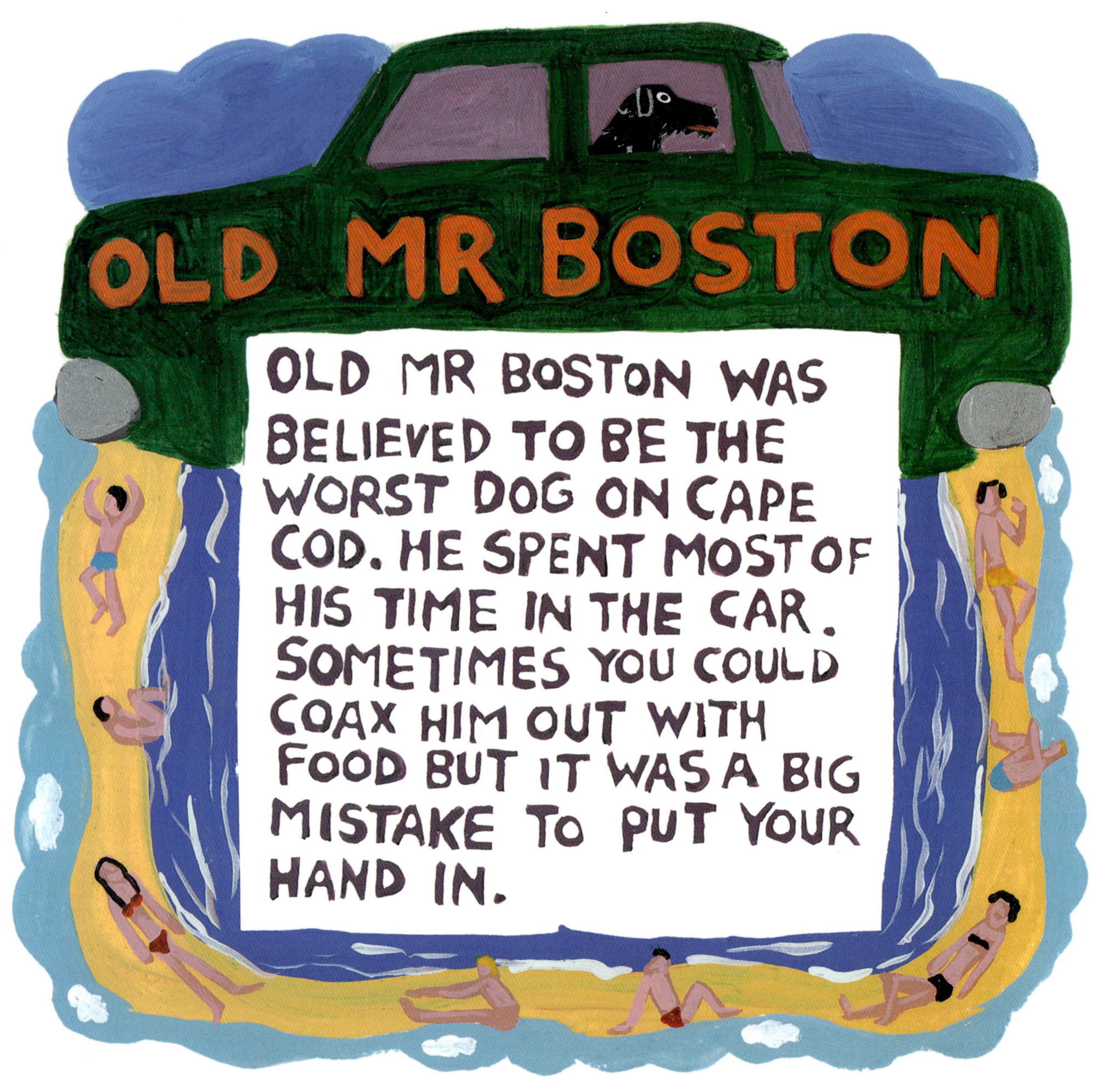
OLD MR BOSTON
OLD MR BOSTON WAS BELIEVED TO BE THE WORST DOG ON CAPE COD. HE SPENT MOST OF HIS TIME IN THE CAR. SOMETIMES YOU COULD COAX HIM OUT WITH FOOD BUT IT WAS A BIG MISTAKE TO PUT YOUR HAND IN.

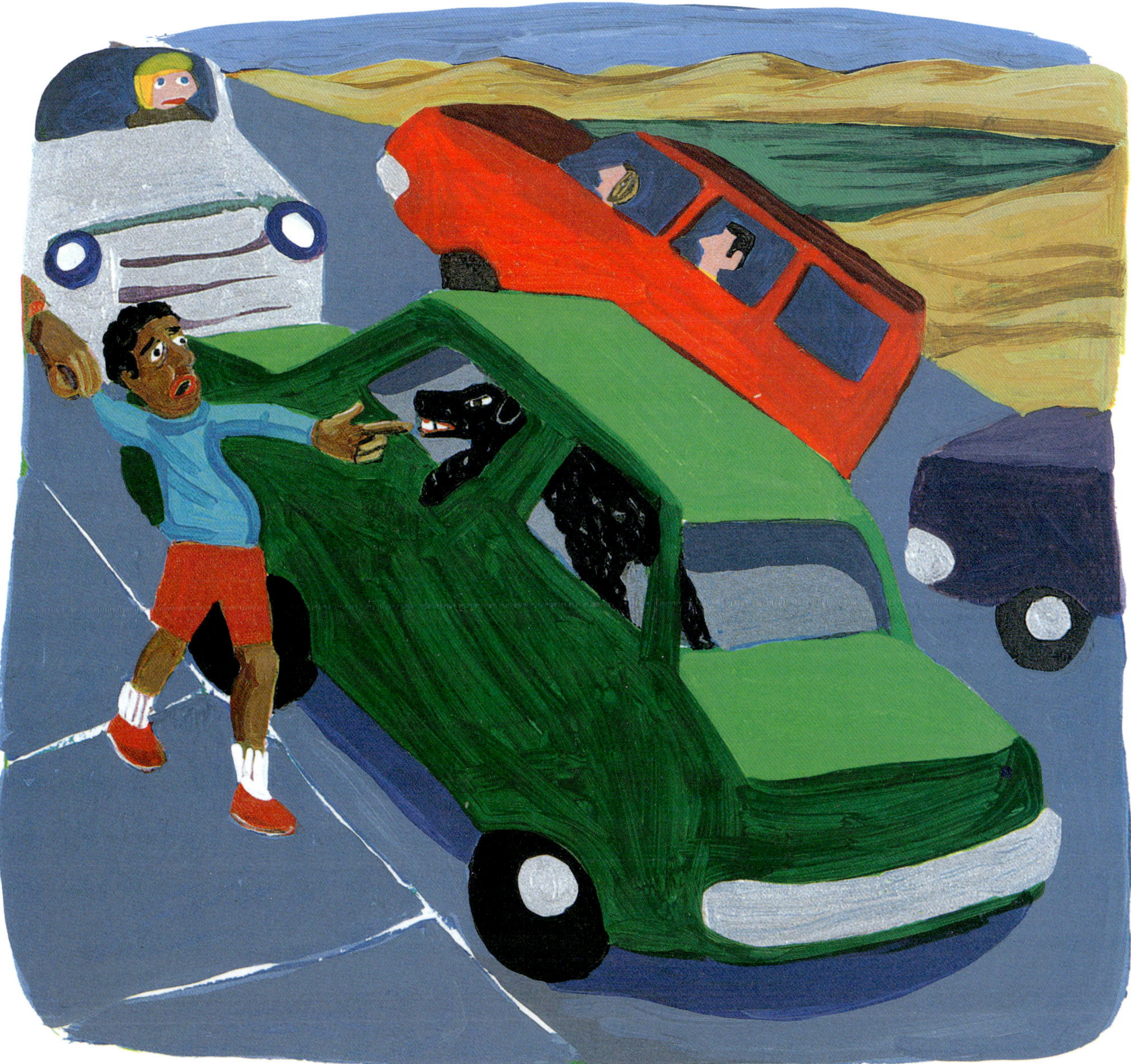

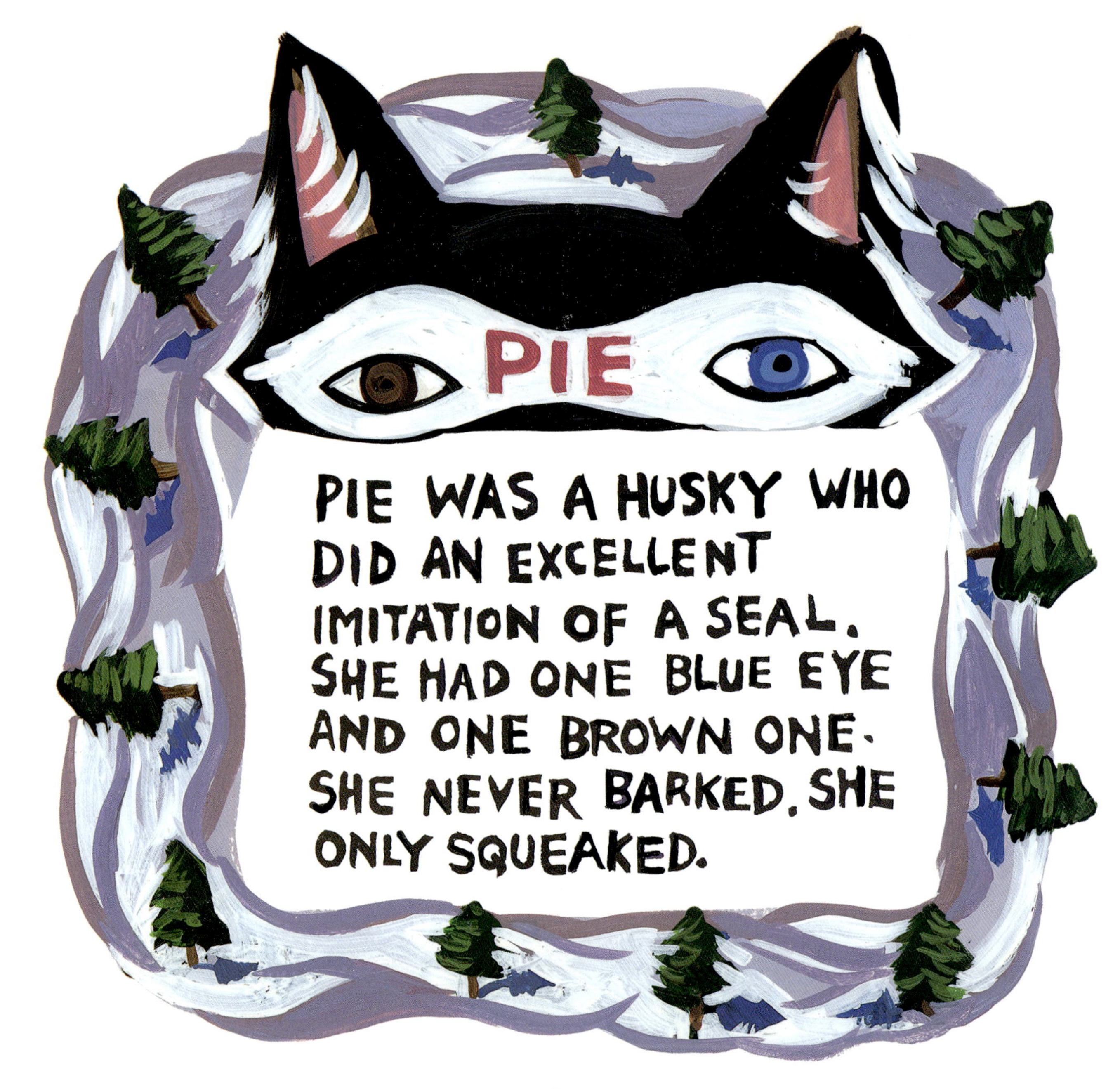
PIE
PIE WAS A HUSKY WHO DID AN EXCELLENT IMITATION OF A SEAL. SHE HAD ONE BLUE EYE AND ONE BROWN ONE. SHE NEVER BARKED. SHE ONLY SQUEAKED.

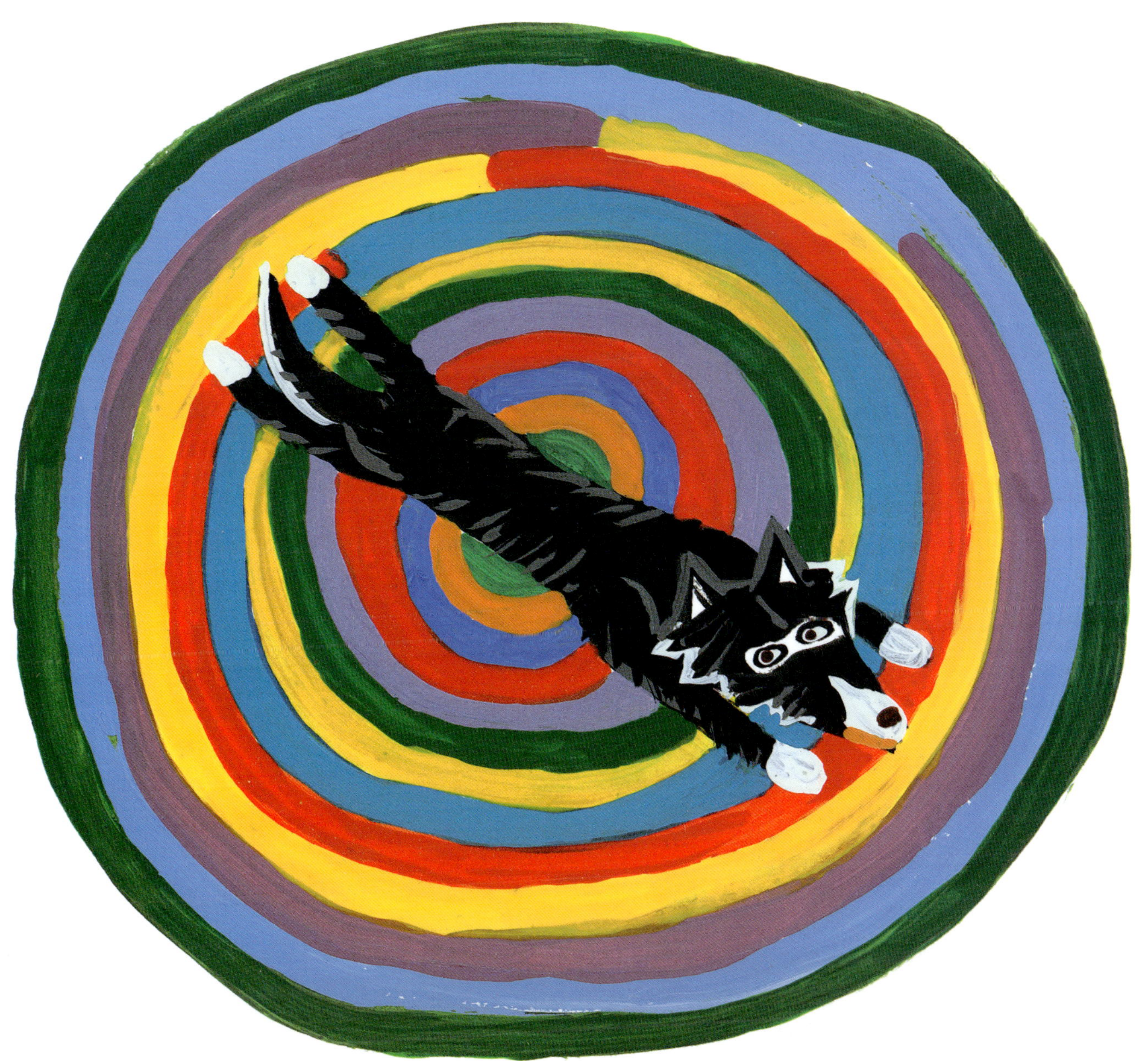

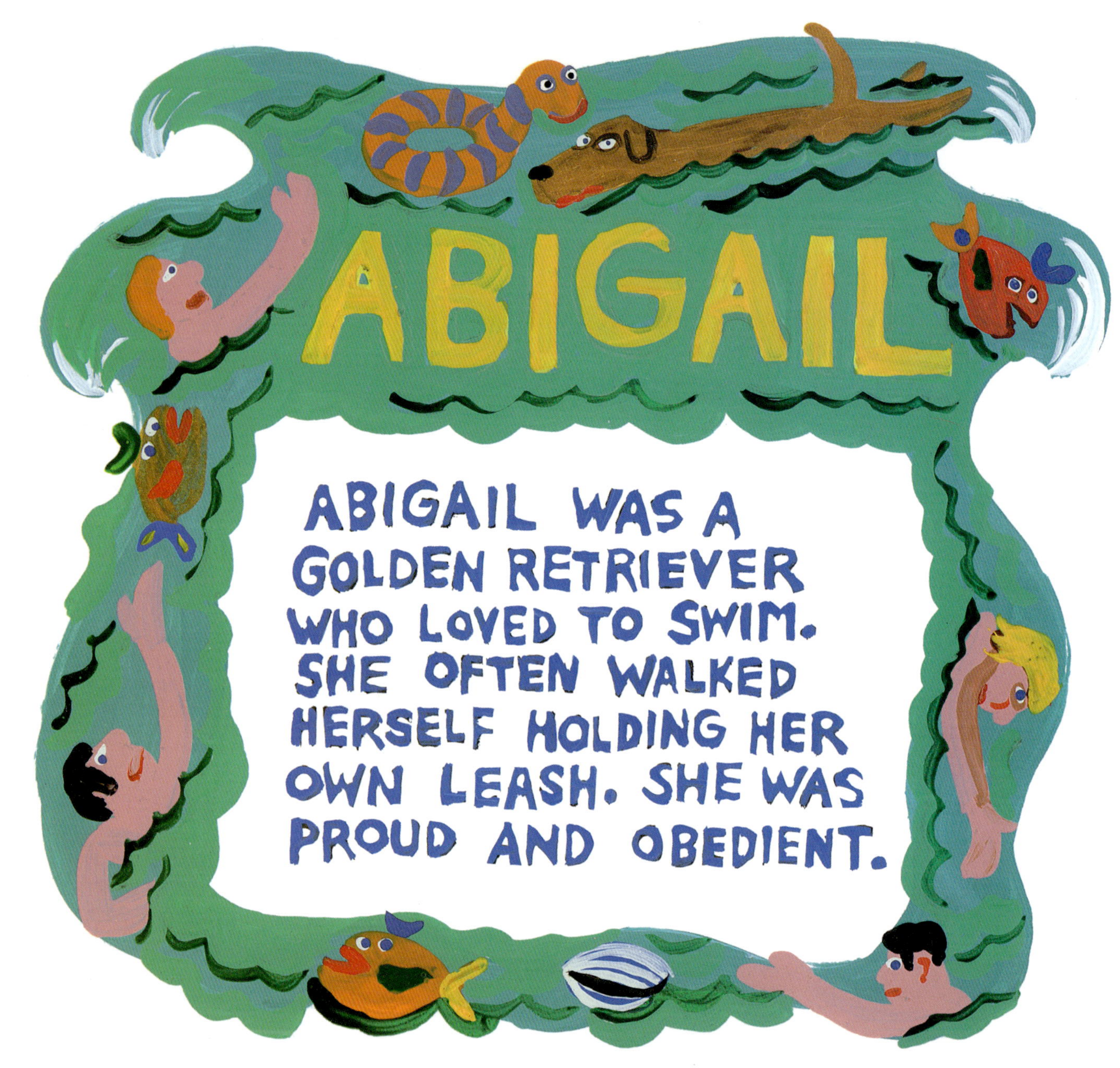
ABIGAIL
ABIGAIL WAS A GOLDEN RETRIEVER WHO LOVED TO SWIM. SHE OFTEN WALKED HERSELF HOLDING HER OWN LEASH. SHE WAS PROUD AND OBEDIENT.

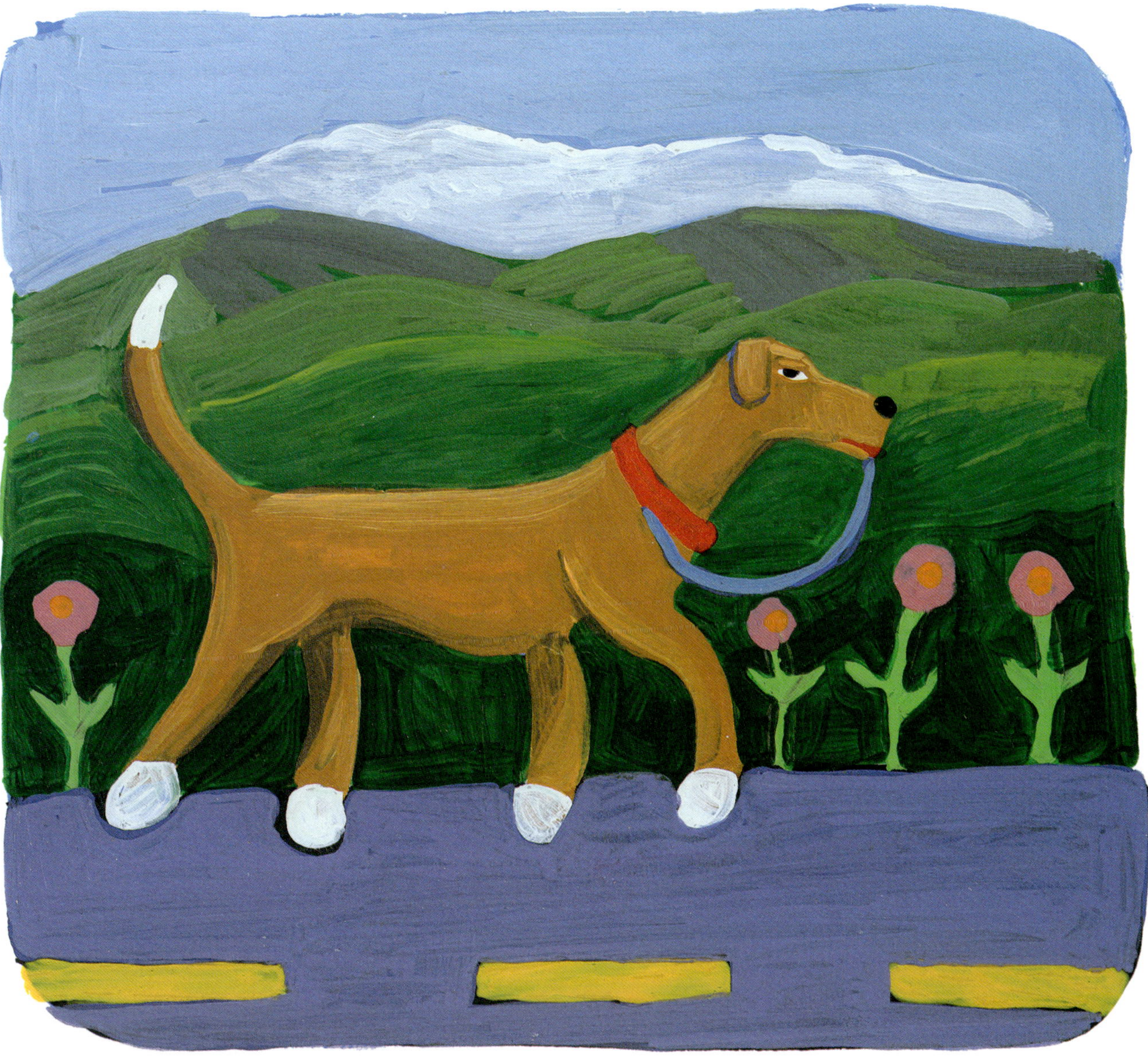

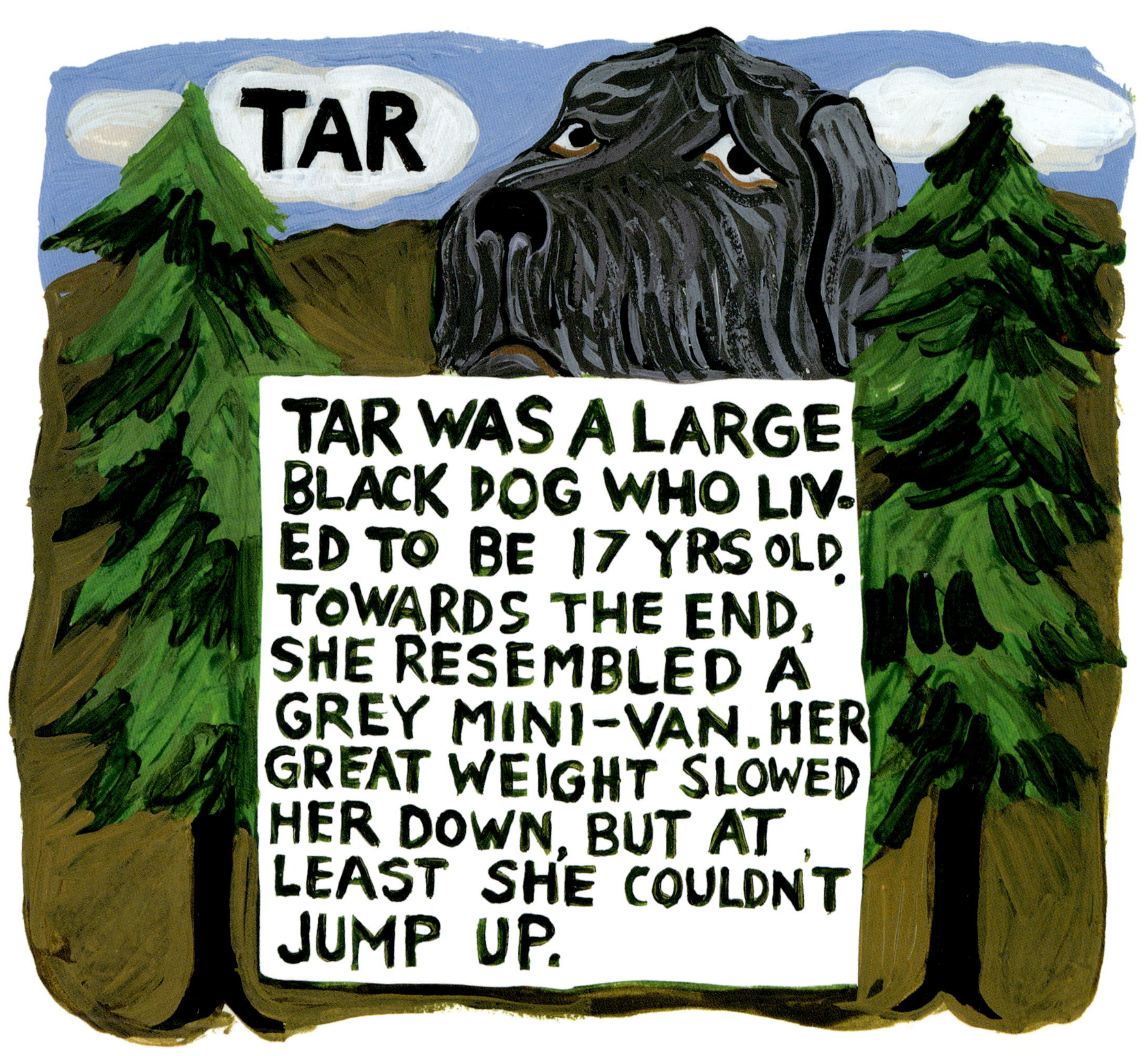
TAR
TAR WAS A LARGE BLACK DOG WHO LIV-ED TO BE 17 YRS OLD. TOWARDS THE END, SHE RESEMBLED A GREY MINI-VAN. HER GREAT WEIGHT SLOWED HER DOWN, BUT AT LEAST SHE COULDN'T JUMP UP.

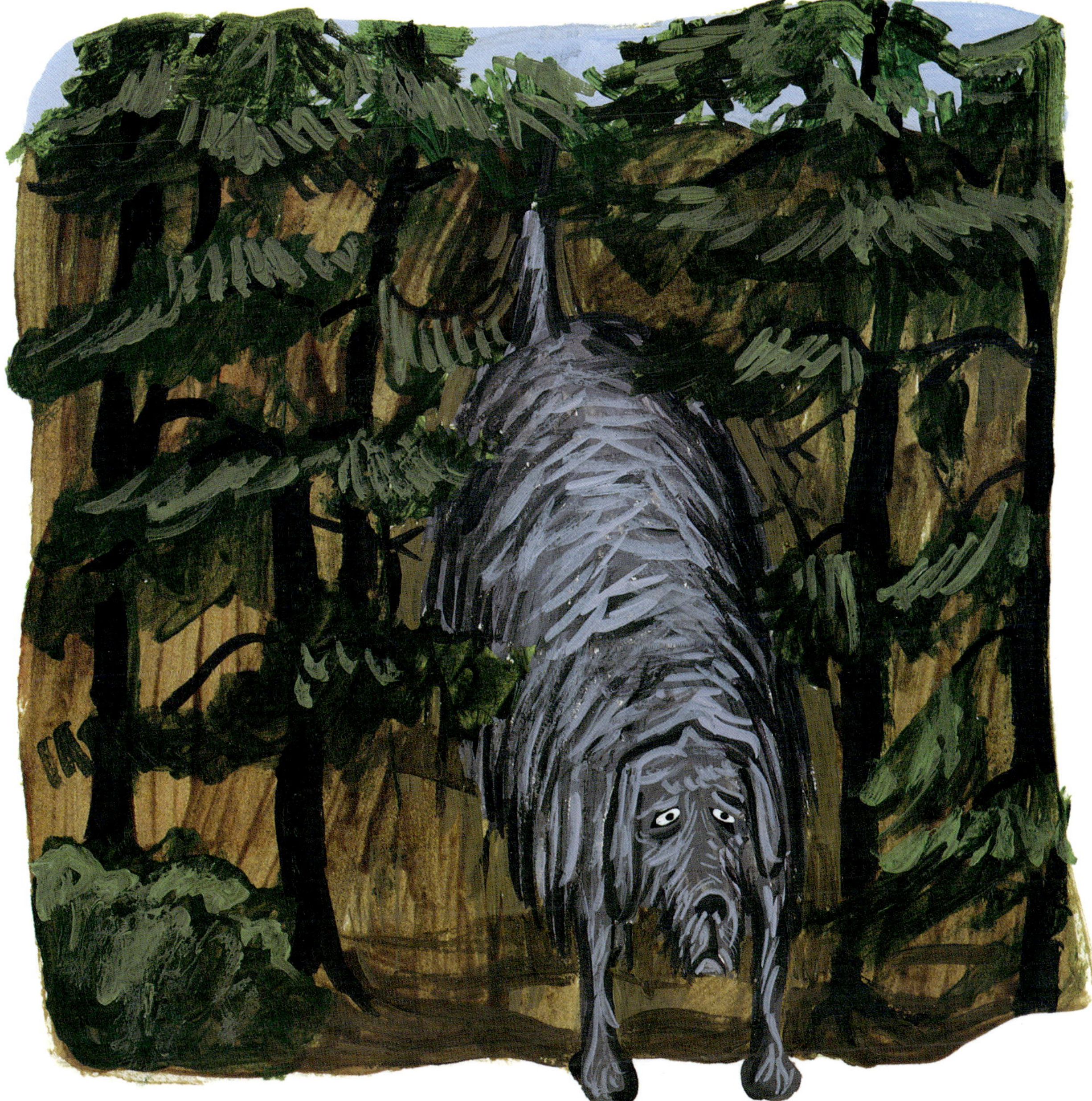

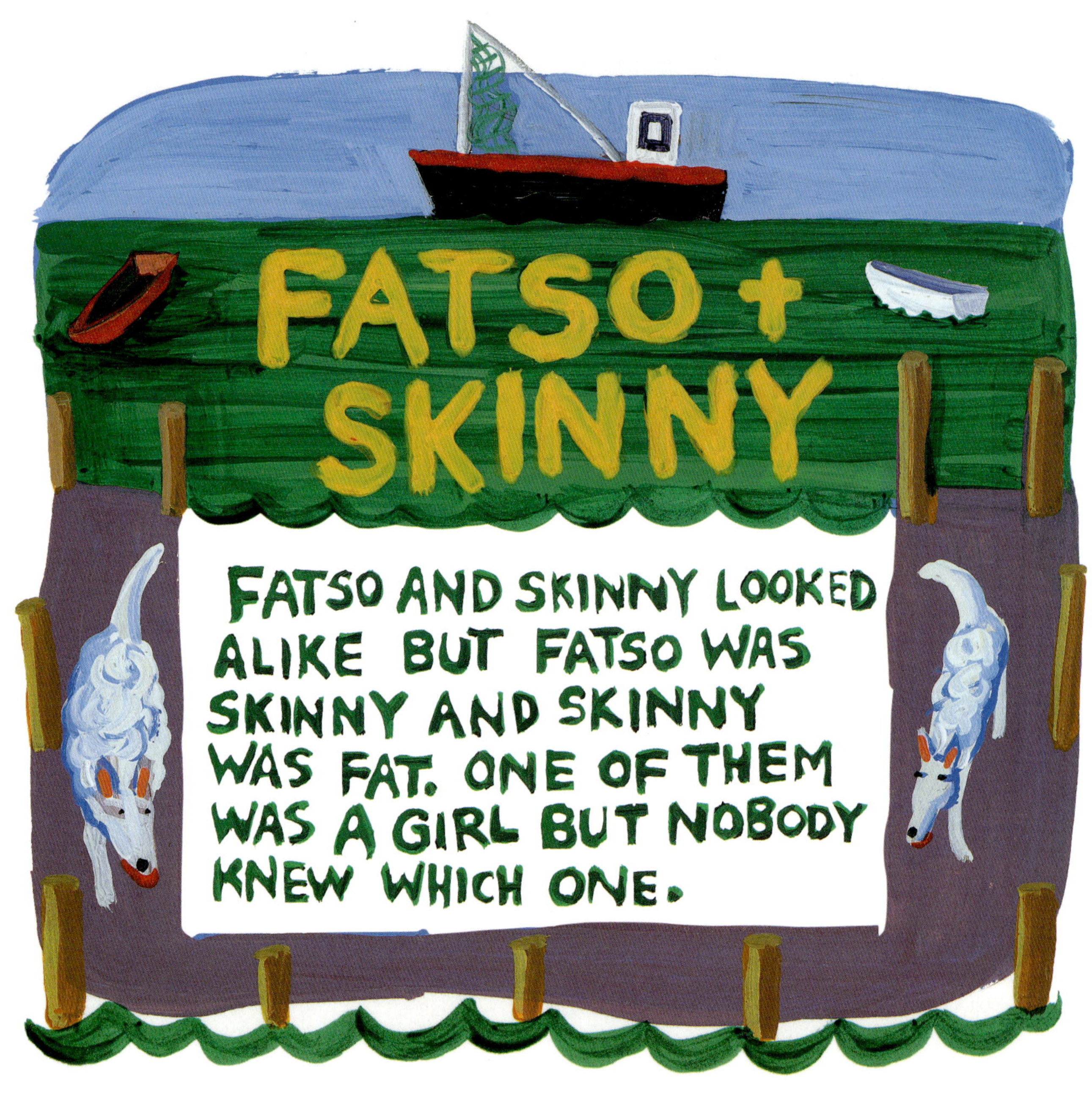
FATSO + SKINNY
FATSO AND SKINNY LOOKED ALIKE BUT FATSO WAS SKINNY AND SKINNY WAS FAT. ONE OF THEM WAS A GIRL BUT NOBODY KNEW WHICH ONE.

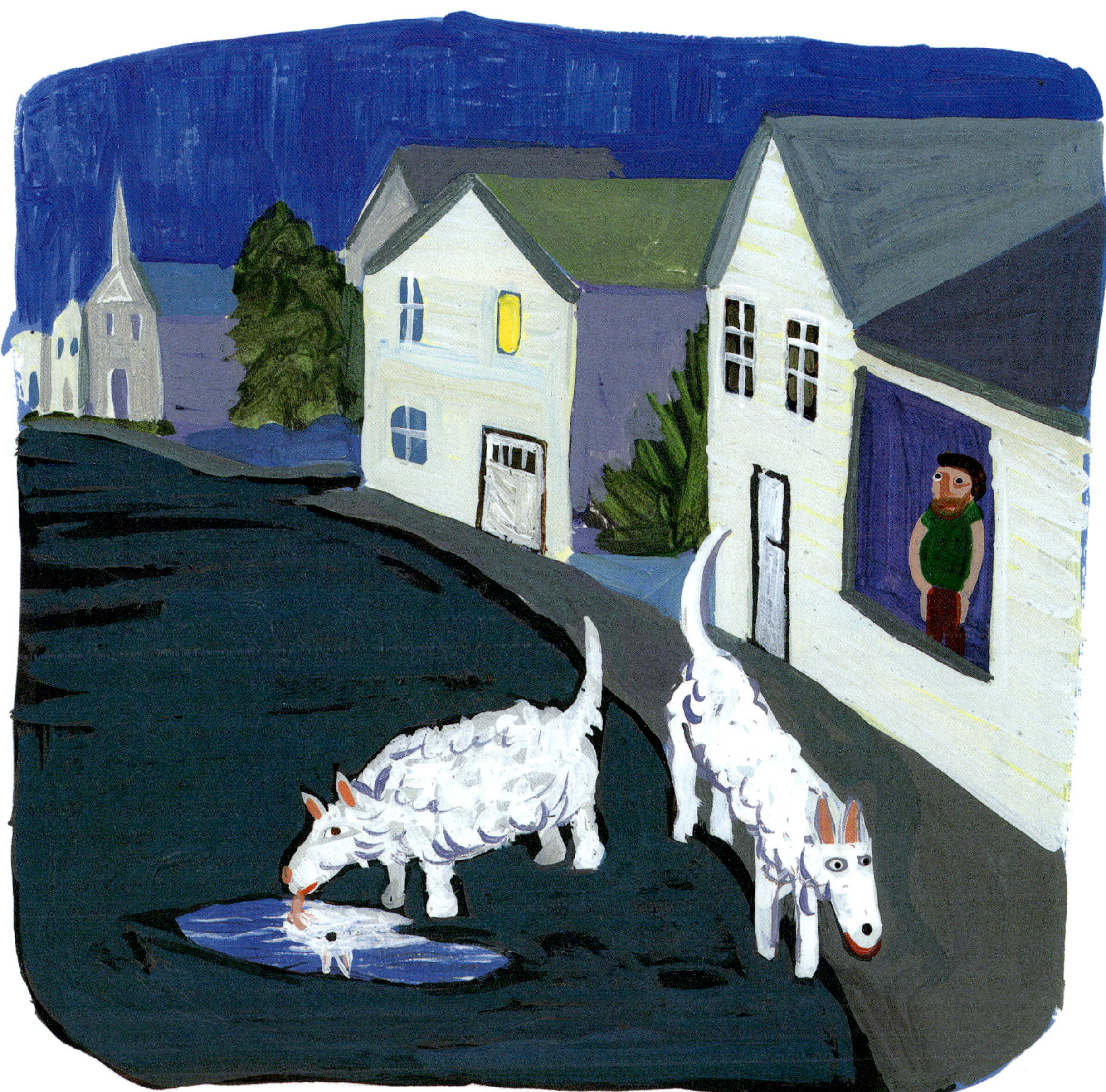

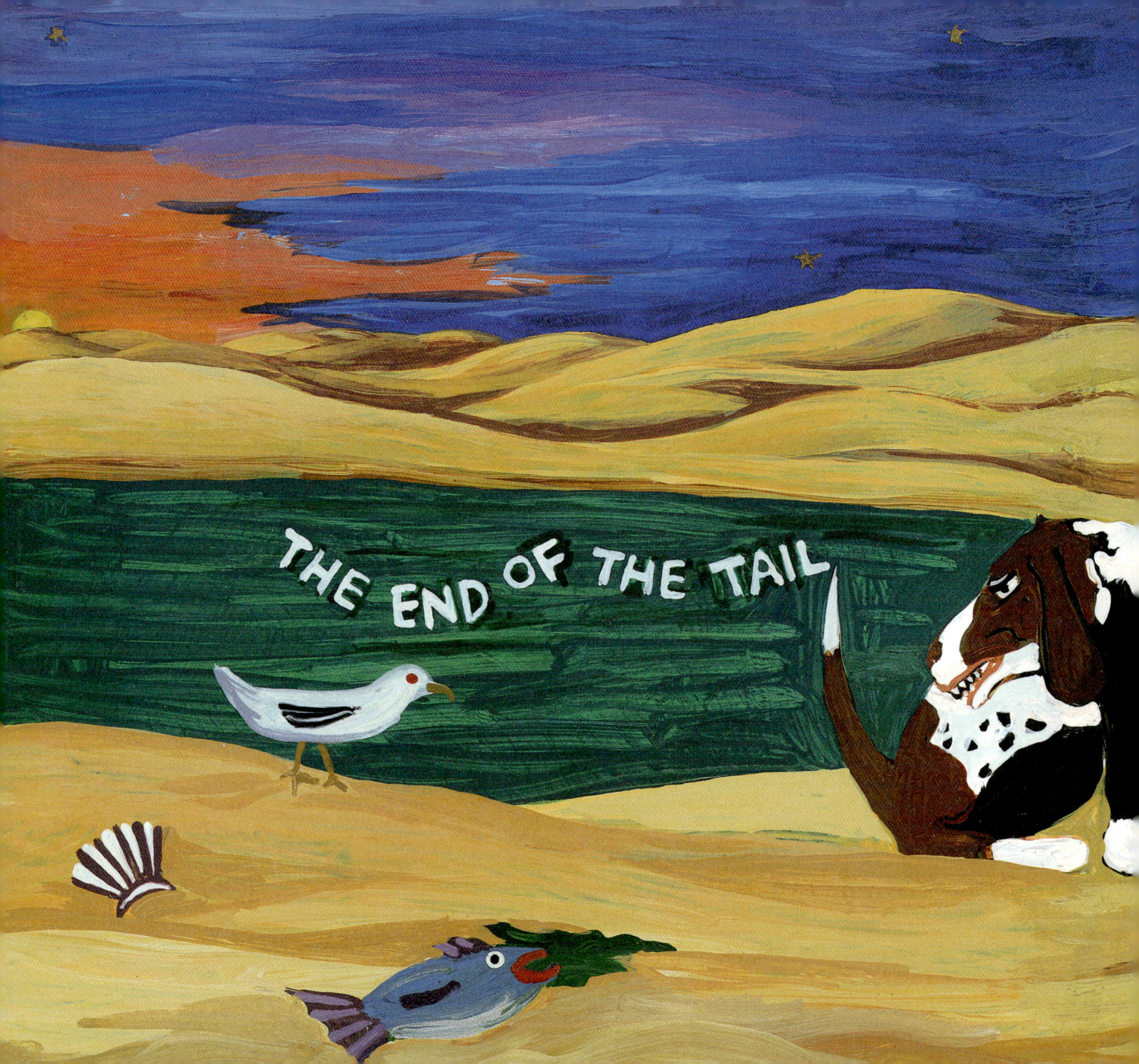
THE END OF THE TAIL

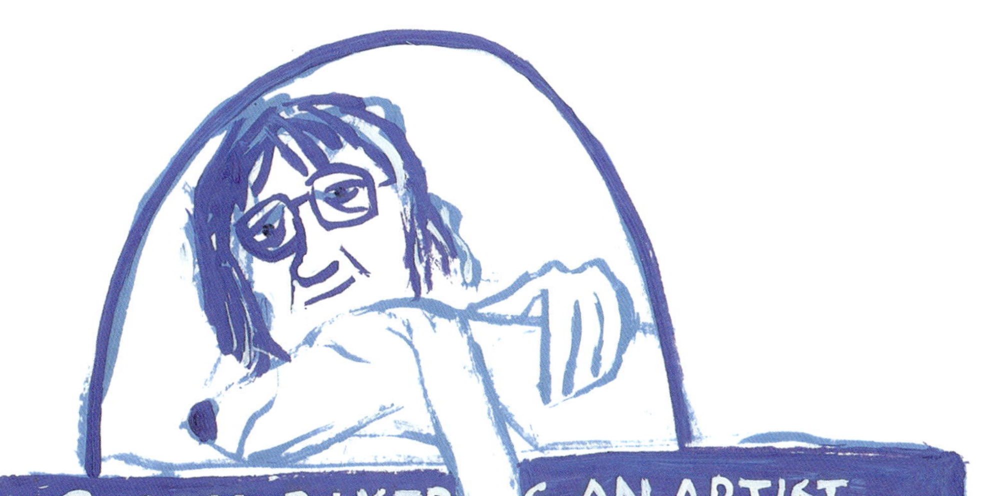

SUSAN BAKER IS AN ARTIST, WRITER AND DOGAHOLIC WHO LIVES ON CAPE COD WITH HER HUSBAND POET KEITH ALTHAUS, HER SON ELLERY AND HER BASSET HOUND STOGIE. SHE GRADUATED FROM RISD IN 1968 AND RECEIVED A FELLOWSHIP FROM THE FINE ARTS WORK CENTER IN PROVINCETOWN IN 1969. HER FIRST BOOK IS CALLED "THE HISTORY OF PROVINCETOWN."

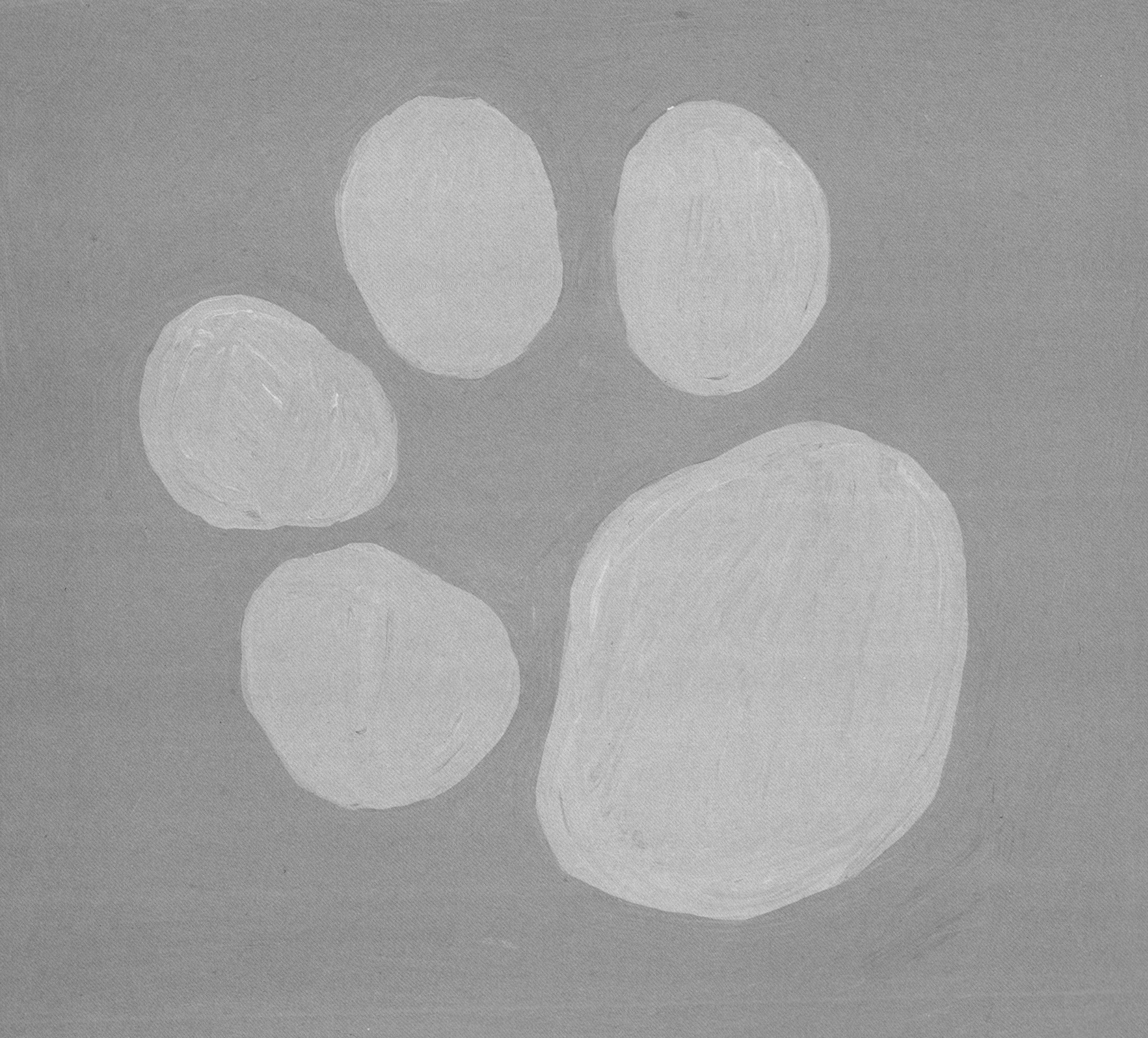